BEYOND THE BASICS

by
David A. DeWitt

MOODY PRESS
CHICAGO

All Scripture quotations in this book are from the *New American Standard
Bible*, © 1960, 1962, 1963, 1968, 1971, 1972, 1973, 1975, and 1977 by The
Lockman Foundation, and are used by permission.

Library of Congress Cataloging in Publication Data

DeWitt, David A.
    Beyond the basics.

    1. Theology, Doctrinal. 2. Evangelicalism.
I. Title.
BT77.D399   1983   230'.044   82-20911
ISBN 0-8024-0178-3

1 2 3 4 5 6 Printing/GB/Year 87 86 85 84 83

Printed in the United States of America

BEYOND THE BASICS

Contents

Introduction

"Hello."

"Janice?"

"Yes."

"This is Margie."

"Oh, hi, Margie."

"You busy? Am I interrupting anything?"

"No, of course not." Janice injected an enthusiasm she didn't feel into her telephone voice. Her eyes strayed to the mound of laundry she was folding. *Oh, well. I really didn't want to do that, anyway*, she thought.

"I've got a question," Margie continued. "Well, actually, I've got lots of questions."

"About what?" Janice inquired.

"I really enjoy your women's Bible study, but to tell you the truth—and please don't think I'm being critical—it sometimes raises more questions in my mind than it answers."

"Really! Like what?"

"Well, it just seems like since I've become a Christian and started coming to Bible study, I have more questions than ever."

"Believe me, Margie, I know just how you feel. Would you mind telling me what some of those questions are?"

"Oh," Margie began, "for example, today we studied prayer. But if God predetermined everything, then what good are my prayers? And why do I feel so guilty all the time? It sure doesn't seem to me like I'm getting any better. My sister and her husband say that I'll lose my salvation if I keep sinning. Is that

7

true? I'm starting to worry about it. Really, Janice, that study guide we're using is great, but I have a bunch of questions it just doesn't answer."

Have you ever been in Janice's spot? I have.

For years now I have been working with new believers, helping them through their early struggles with Christianity. I have used all sorts of different material, too, but I must agree with Margie that most material for new Christians leaves a lot of questions unanswered. The "basics" are generally covered— prayer, Bible study, witnessing, how to study and apply God's Word to your life. And those are the things that *should* be covered with new believers. I have found, however, that a number of other questions inevitably pops up en route. In this book I have answered the eight questions I have found most frequently asked by new believers as they work their way through those "basics."

I will not attempt to exhaust any of these subjects, nor to debate them in every detail. If someone wishes to study any of them exhaustively, this book may serve as an easy-to-read introduction, but that's all.

However, if someone wishing to study the Bible has a gnawing curiosity about one of the issues considered here, yet finds himself without the time to pursue an exhaustive, technically-oriented investigation of the subject—this book will help. I have attempted to pursue a logical, reasonable, and (most important) biblical approach to these sometimes difficult areas without demanding an understanding of technical jargon.

Each chapter begins with a conversational situation. The reason for that is not simply to make the book more readable, but to make a specific point. The conversational situations are all real. They are actual ministry situations. I include them to emphasize the fact that ministry is not restricted to something that happens in a meeting. I hope that when the reader begins to learn the Bible's answers to questions such as these, he or she will begin to use them in similar situations.

1

Is There a Conflict Between Creation and Evolution?

"Any questions?"

There was a long period of silence. Jim stirred restlessly in his seat. He had lots of questions. But he didn't feel like asking them in this lecture class of over four hundred students.

"Are there any questions at all?" Professor Elizabeth Carlson (not her real name) repeated. She had been teaching Biology 103 at the university for several years now, so she was confident that she could handle any questions a sophomore might ask. She had just finished her standard lecture on the basics of evolutionary biology and was about to go on to the next part of the syllabus when Jim nervously stood to his feet.

"Umm—well—ahh—Dr. Carlson, are you saying that evolution within a given species is proof of evolution from one species to another?"

"I am certainly saying it is great evidence for it," Professor Carlson answered.

"Actually, though, there is only evidence for evolution within a species and none at all for something evolving from one species to another, is that right?"

Jim's question was not that of an antagonistic creationist trying to prove a point. He really wanted to know. He was an atheist—well, maybe a part-time atheist. Usually he was not sure whether God existed, but sometimes he was sure He did *not*.

"Oh, I would say there is lots of evidence for it," returned Dr. Carlson. She then reminded Jim of all the material she had just presented on embryos, vestigial organs, fossils, ancient dates, mutations, natural selection, laboratory experiments, and geological formations.

Jim had not yet researched any of those things for himself, but he did have some more basic questions bothering him.

"Well, then, where would you say the original life came from?" he asked.

"From a non-living prehistoric bed of chemicals," the professor answered.

"I thought we learned that Pasteur proved that life never comes from non-living things," Jim said.

"Well, this is different," she returned. "Generally it doesn't, but sometime in the past after a long period of time it did."

"Then why did evolution stop?" Jim wanted to know.

"It didn't," Dr. Carlson insisted, with a slight edge to her voice.

"Then where are all the half-apes on their way toward becoming humans and all the half-reptiles on their way toward becoming birds, or whatever? It seems to me that, if evolution were still going on, every creature would be in the process of becoming a higher one. We ought to be able to put a monkey at one end of a football field and a man at the other, with every link between them. *Then* we would have evidence that changes are now going on."

"But these changes take millions of years," she patiently reminded Jim.

"However long it takes, we ought to be able to see some evidence of that evolutionary process between species if, as you say, it is still going on. But as far as I can see, we are being asked to accept evolution between species on faith because—"

Jim was interrupted by the loud buzzer that ended the hour.

CREATION OR EVOLUTION?

Professor Carlson chose not to pursue the issue at the next class. But Jim pursued it. He discussed it for several years with professors of biology, chemistry, biochemistry, physics, and geology, both evolutionists and creationists. Here is an outline of what he found.

CATEGORIES OF EVOLUTION

Evolution can be put into two categories—that which takes place *within* a certain kind of life form and that which takes place *between* two different ones. The word *kind* is probably better than the word *species*. For one thing, *species* is a subcategory of *kind*, and people today have trouble defining what constitutes *species*. Different varieties of plants and animals can be produced, but no one has ever produced a life form of a different kind. The Bible says nothing about species, but it does say that each group God created was to reproduce "after its kind" (Genesis 1:11-21). So, evolutionary changes within kinds is quite consistent with the Bible, but the idea of evolution of life forms from one kind to another is something that must be carefully evaluated.

From here on, for the sake of simplicity, let's use the word *evolution* only to refer to the theory that all the *kinds* of life slowly developed from one common life form, which itself developed from an ocean of non-living chemicals in the earth's distant past.

ZERO OBSERVATIONS

The major problem with this type of evolution is that there are no observations of it. Many facts can, of course, be observed in nature, but the question is, "Is evolution the best, or even a reasonable, explanation of them?"

In order to accept evolution as true, we must have faith in a philosophy or religious theory that is without observation. As Henry Morris put it, "Thus the evolutionist has to resort to an explanation in terms of an imaginary atmosphere which no longer exists, an imaginary ocean composition which no longer exists, and hypothetical processes which no longer exist, to explain the evolution of primitive organisms which no longer exist: Whatever philosophic or religious value such speculations might have, they are certainly not *scientific*."[1]

ARGUMENTS MADE FOR EVOLUTION

Some of the subjects that have been suggested to supply evidence for evolution are: embryos, vestigial organs, fossils, ancient dates, mutations, natural selection, laboratory experiments, and geological formations.

Embryos. As an embryo develops, it was (and I say "was" because this has largely been rejected) supposed to repeat the stages of the evolutionary history of the creature. For example, the human embryo looks as if it has fish gills at one point. Of course, the observation of the development of an embryo is only evidence for the development of an embryo. It is not the observation of one creature developing into another, but simply the stages of development of one creature. Any assumption that these stages are symbolic of evolution is speculation made on religion or philosophy, and not on science.

Vestigial organs. Vestigial organs are those organs that supposedly have no function—sort of evolutionary leftovers. They presumably had a function in our past, but have none today. One hundred and eighty such organs were once listed in man. In reality, there is no conclusive evidence that any organs are useless.[2] The appendix, for example, once thought to be useless, now seems to have a definite protective function, especially in infants.

Fossils. Fossils are supposed to demonstrate evolution by giving us examples of our prehistoric past. The truth is, the fossil

1. Henry Morris, *The Bible and Modern Science* (Chicago: Moody, 1951), p. 34.
2. Kenneth Boa, *Creation or Evolution?* (Atlanta: Walk Thru the Bible Media Ministries, 1980), p. 16.

evidence could never be used to prove evolution unless evolution was already assumed to be true by people faithfully devoted to it as a concept. To claim fossils as evidence is comparable to saying the earth is flat because the pieces of it that I can see from my office window look flat. That would only be evidence if I already believed it and was looking for something to prove my philosophy.

Speculative pictures in textbooks give us the misleading impression that the fossil record presents a clear, unbroken chain, linking modern man with an apelike ancestor. We're led to believe that an artist has simply "fleshed out" the prehistoric fossils we have. But such is not the case. In reality, all we have are a few ape bones, a few human bones, and a lot of religious imagination. A list of the actual fossil evidence is included in Appendix 2 of this book.

Diseases like arthritis and rickets cause similar variations and always have. If we could examine the skeletons of the apes and humans who die today, we would find many malformed skeletons. If we took an average group of people on any city street during the lunch hour, put hair all over some of the more stooped-over ones, moppy wigs on some, and business suits on the rest, we would have the same "evidence" we see in evolution textbooks.

But what is it evidence of? It is evidence that there are different shaped people—that's all. Since many "normal" skeletons were discovered near the supposed prehistoric ones, it seems as though it would make more sense simply to suppose that man always looked something like he does today with the same amount of variations.[3]

Ancient dates. Every so often evolutionists turn up a fossil to which they assign an ancient date. On your summer vacation you may visit a cave or rock formation, which the guide tells you is so

3. Thomas F. Heinze, *Creation vs. Evolution Handbook* (Grand Rapids: Baker, 1973), pp. 59-60.

many millions of years old. How do they know that? I used to think there was some proved accurate method—which I could never understand—for determining those dates. Then I started asking questions. Here's what I learned.

There are basically two types of dating (with lots of variations, of course): uranium dating and carbon dating. Uranium dating is for rock-type things, and carbon dating is for previously living things (like bones).

First a word about uranium dating. The accuracy of both methods has been questioned lately, but if we suppose uranium dating to be accurate, then it provides a way to date rocks, not bones. Also, if there was a creation, then the process only provides a way to date rocks back as far as that creation. If the world was created from nothing in six twenty-four hour days, and if it was made with the apparent "age" necessary for all forms of life to continue, then it would date millions of years old on the sixth twenty-four hour day.

Creating things with the appearance of age is common to God's work, anyway. God the Son created the world (John 1:1-3; Colossians 1:16-17). When that same Son of God did miracles in Galilee, He often created things with the appearance of age. For example, when He fed the five thousand (Matthew 14; Mark 6; Luke 9) with five loaves and two fish, He created fish and bread with the appearance of age. They were not baby fish or uncooked loaves. Even though only seconds old, they were in the form of what any other bread or fish would be after the appropriate time of natural aging.

Carbon dating is used for bones and other fossils. But its accuracy can only be trusted back a few thousand years. *Popular Science* magazine recently reported that activity on the surface of the sun, which varies from year to year, greatly affects radiocarbon dating. Even so, most scientists figure they have a pretty accurate guess back to eight thousand years.

"But beyond 8,000 years?" Says the University of Rochester's Grove: "There is no way to adjust. When I say that the woolly mammoth we dated is 26,000 years old, I can determine possible error based on reproductibility, but God knows what the cosmic rays were like back around that time."[4]

So the dating methods are not used by evolutionists to *prove* anything. They use them to establish particular dates for things they have already assumed to be very old.

Mutation and natural selection. Mutants, and the natural selection of mutants with a greater capacity to survive, have been offered as an explanation for how evolution works. The problem is that almost all observed mutations are detrimental, not helpful (for example, clubfootedness and retardation). Living cells by their very nature do not reproduce anything more organized than themselves. In other words, we notice once again that the evolutionary explanation requires faith of a religious or philosophical sort.

Laboratory experiments. Many "interesting" results have been observed under laboratory conditions. Rats with straight tails have been bred into rats with curly tails. Chemicals have been so arranged as to produce reactions similar to those in the basic fluids of the living cells. This is supposed to be evidence in favor of animals evolving and life coming from non-life in nature.

But that is not natural selection—that is *laboratory* selection. Suppose we let those rats go in the city dump, then what do we observe? Ordinary rats, that's what. What if we dump that chemical substance that is supposed to produce life into a Mississippi swamp or a mud puddle, then what will we observe? Nothing more than we would observe looking at any swamp water or mud puddle! The point is, laboratory selection is not natural selection. What it *is* evidence for is that it takes the direction and purpose of the experimenter to produce anything at all different from nature's status quo. The reasonable conclusion is that anything created requires a creator.

4. Robert Gannon, "How Old Is It?—The Elegant Science of Dating Objects," *Popular Science*, November 1979, p. 79.

Geological formations. Glaciers move slowly; rivers cut their beds slowly; oil forms slowly; and so on. Evolution points to those processes as evidence that the earth is very old, having formed over aeons of time. But the fact that geological formations change slowly says nothing about how they were formed originally.

When I look at the little stream that runs through my neighborhood I notice some little sandbars on its edges—especially when it curves. But the water is almost clear. Suppose I ask myself, "How long would it take that water to deposit those sandbars?" Since there is very little sand or silt being carried along and deposited by the stream, I would conclude that it might take hundreds or even thousands of years.

However, if I looked at that same stream after one of our Texas gully-washer rainstorms, I would see water mucky with sand and silt. Often there is enough to deposit those sandbars in one afternoon.

What is my point? Just because things are changing slowly as we observe them now does not mean they formed slowly originally. So the fact that things change slowly as we look at them does not mean that they are very old.

If the earth was created as the Bible says, and if there was a universal flood and upheaval such as occurred at the time of Noah—even to the extent of rearranging the continents—then all these slowly changing formations would have been set in motion by two big events: creation and the Flood.

BASIC PROBLEMS WITH EVOLUTION

Not only are there serious questions about the evidence used to promote evolution, but there are also some problems with the basic idea.

Spontaneous generation. One such basic question is: "Where did everything come from?" This question has two parts: "Where did life come from?" and, "Where did the substances that life came from, come from?"

The only possible evolutionist answer to the "life" question is that it spontaneously generated itself from nonliving things. Not only did Pasteur prove that to be false, but even more significantly, we have zero evidence of it. Nobody—at any time, under any conditions—has ever observed a living thing coming from nonliving things.

Besides the problem of life coming from nonlife, the evolutionist must assume that the nonliving material comes from nothing. This problem is, of course, the same. No one has *ever* observed something coming from nothing.

Intermediate life forms. The search for some "missing link" falls infinitely short of what is needed to provide observable evidence for evolution. If evolution is a fact of nature, new kinds of life should be evolving all the time. We should be able to put a man on the equator of the earth, with an ape next to him, and then fill in every link between the two, all around the equator. There should be no distinguishable spaces at all, since every lower form would be evolving a creature toward the next higher form. Even if some group were wiped out somewhere, it would be replaced by an ever-evolving process. It should be completely impossible to distinguish "kinds" of plants or animals, since each one would be evolving another one almost like it with a little better survival value.

Where are all the millions of creatures that are part-fish, part-reptiles (if that's what they evolved into)? And where are all the millions of creatures that are part-reptile, part-bird, part-ape, and part-human? The truth is there are fish, reptiles, birds, apes, and humans. But there is not one single life form that has any chain of creatures between it and any other life form. Instead, each of them reproduces only one observable way— after its own kind. (See Genesis 1:11-12, 21-22.)

The Bible and evolution. People who take the Bible at face value realize that there is a difference between its teachings and those of the evolutionist. It has become popular, however, to try to wed the two. That is done by assuming God created everything from nothing and then directed it along on an evolutionary path. The six days of creation are seen as six very long ages, which lead up to modern man as we know him.

That view has, however, some very serious problems.

For one thing, the order of events is all wrong. Evolution claims that living organisms originated in the sea millions of years before plants appeared. But the Bible tells us that grasses, seed-bearing plants, and trees were all created on the third day. Sea life, however, was not created until the fifth day. The Bible also says that the fish and sea creatures were created the same day as the birds; evolution says they were ages apart. The Scripture teaches that creeping things like insects were among the last things created, yet evolution says they were among the first. Besides this, the sun and moon were not set in the sky until the fourth day. That would be devastating to the plants created on the third day if the time span were much longer than twenty-four hours. Even if we understand the days to be ages, the Bible runs contrary to evolution. To be reasonable we must assume one or the other to be wrong.

Besides the fact that the biblical order of events contradicts the evolutionary order, there is a second problem for anyone who believes the Bible. The Hebrew word for "day" in the Genesis creation account is used the same way as our English word for it. Whenever this word appears with a numerical word like "first" or "second," as it does in Genesis, it always refers to a literal day. Besides that, there is a different Hebrew word for "age," or "long period of time," which would have been the one to use here, if that's what God meant.[5]

There is a third problem. The Bible tells us that death started when the first two human beings sinned (Romans 5:12-14). Although only man is named, it seems most reasonable to

---

5. Henry M. Morris, *The Bible and Modern Science* (Chicago: Moody, 1951), p. 29.

conclude that no creature had died before Adam and Eve sinned—not even animals (Jeremiah 12:4; Romans 8:20). Evolution, however, tells us that there were millions of years' worth of skeletons in the ground before man appeared. Since the Bible says that all six days of creation were completed before any living creature died, it would not help to interpret the days as ages; that would mean six ages (of whatever length they were) passed without any animal or man dying.

A fourth consideration is the teaching about creation throughout the Bible. Genesis is not the only place in the Bible that needs to be tampered with if we are to accept evolution. In Exodus 20:11, Moses writes, "For in six days the LORD made the heavens and the earth, the sea and all that is in them, and rested on the seventh day." This was given as an example for Israel to rest on the seventh day. Since this meant that they were to rest for the normal working part of a twenty-four hour day—not an age or indefinite period of time—it would be reasonable to assume that this passage also meant God created the world in six literal days.

God did not seem to have had any evolutionary process in mind when He spoke through Isaiah, saying, "It is I who made the earth, and created man upon it" (Isaiah 45:12). Jesus Christ emphasized His teaching on marriage by claiming, "He who created them from the beginning MADE THEM MALE AND FEMALE" (Matthew 19:4). That would be a strange way to put it, if man had evolved slowly from a single cell.

The apostle Paul says that it is God who "calls into being that which does not exist" (Romans 4:17). "For it was Adam who was first created, and then Eve" (1 Timothy 2:13). Those statements are pretty hard to fit into an evolutionary mold.

The apostle John wrote, "Worthy art Thou, our Lord and our God, to receive glory and honor and power; for Thou didst create all things, and because of Thy will they existed, and were created" (Revelation 4:11).

A fifth problem with evolution for the biblical Christian concerns the doctrine of sin. The Bible teaches that sin entered the world through the disobedience of the first man, Adam (Genesis 3:1-7; Romans 5:12). Because of that sin, suffering also entered the world. The whole creation was cursed or lowered to a condition where even nature itself was balanced through suffering (Genesis 3:14-19; Romans 8:22). The Bible also teaches that God did not want us to suffer. He created a perfect world, the Garden of Eden, for people to live in. Suffering is the result of man's sin.

On the other hand, if God caused the world to evolve slowly to its present state, then He is indeed a bad God. He is not to be looked to for any kind of happiness, since He wanted this to be a suffering world. If we have a world that has evolved into what God wanted, then God must have intended for us to suffer. What hope would there be in turning to such a God for peace, joy, and salvation? What peace—the turmoil we now know and the cruelty we observe in nature? Salvation to what—an existence such as we see in this world?

But if the world was created in six literal days and it was the Garden of Eden described in Genesis, then we have a God who desires a world without suffering. We then have good reason to believe Him when He says concerning those who return to Him, "He shall wipe away every tear from their eyes; and there shall no longer be any death; there shall no longer be any mourning, or crying, or pain" (Revelation 21:4).

Furthermore, if there were no literal Adam and Eve, then there was no original sin. Thus there is no sin (since it never originated), and therefore we have no need of a Savior. Any attempt to evolutionize the Bible destroys the doctrine of sin and our need for salvation.

SCIENCE AND THE BIBLE

There is no contradiction between true science and the Bible. The word *science* has its root meaning in the word *know*.[6] It

6. Phillip B. Gove, ed., *Webster's Seventh New Collegiate Dictionary* (Springfield, Mass.: Merriam, 1965), p. 1034.

is the attaining and possessing of knowledge. Since the basic way to know things is to observe them, science studies that which is observable. As long as a scientific method deals in repeatable experiments to arrive at laws of nature, it is truly scientific.

Those laws, then, are rules of nature that can be counted on because they can be repeatedly demonstrated and are not disproved by observation. The law of gravity, for example, concludes that the mass of bodies like the earth, moon, or other planets will attract other bodies at or near its surface. There is no observable contradiction to the law of gravity. That's why it is called a law. As long as science deals with these observable laws and builds upon them, then it is always in complete harmony with the Bible.

The First Law of Thermodynamics observes that energy can neither be created nor destroyed. The Bible agrees (Ecclesiastes 1:9; 3:14). The Second Law of Thermodynamics states that the amount of usable energy is running down. The Bible agrees (Romans 8:20). Astronomy observes no end to the billions of stars in billions of galaxies. The Bible agrees (Job 22:12; Isaiah 55:9; Jeremiah 31:37). Astronomy also observes that stars differ greatly from one another and that orbiting bodies—including our own sun—follow a fixed, predictable path. The Bible agrees (Psalm 19:6; Jeremiah 31:35-36; 1 Corinthians 15:41). Science observes that the earth is a sphere not attached to anything and that the moon does not give off its own light. The Bible agrees (Job 25:5; 26:7; Isaiah 40:22). Medical science observed in 1628 that blood circulation is a key to life. The Bible agrees (Leviticus 17:11).

But when scientists begin formulating philosophies like evolution and treating them like laws, then it becomes a type of faith or religion. Some have called it "scientism." It is an "ism," a belief, not an observation of nature. Evolution is not the first theory adhered to by faith. The flat earth theory was also such a belief, as was the theory that life spontaneously generated itself from non-living matter. The Greeks once held the theory that the universe was a big globe rotating around the earth with the stars stuck in its edges. These were theories, not observations. When these, or any unobserved beliefs, become assumptions and are for all practical purposes treated like laws, then what *was* science becomes scientism—a belief. The Bible is in complete harmony with all facts, but not with all beliefs.

So if the case for evolution is without evidence, how about the case for creation? Well, of course, creation is as absent of observation as evolution is. Nobody alive has observed God creating the heaven and the earth. Nor can we observe anything now being created. So creation has to be accepted by faith, just like evolution. The difference is that the creationists are more apt to admit it.

But that is not to say there is no good case for creation. There is, in fact, less blind faith required for creation than for evolution.

Why? Primarily because creationists do not ignore the universal fact that no effect can be greater than its cause, and every effect has an adequate cause. There is no observable contradiction to that truth. Yet the theory of evolution contradicts it. Evolution says intelligence was developed from nonintelligent material, morality evolved from nonmoral processes, emotions came out of unemotional chemicals, extremely complex molecules arose out of simple structures and so on. All of that contradicts the basic fact of cause and effect.

Creationism, on the other hand, is completely consistent with cause and effect. We *can* observe, for example, that the universe: (1) is complex, (2) is seemingly infinite or unending in size, (3) is not eternal (that is, everything deteriorates), (4) has never been observed to create anything, (5) has order and design or beauty, (6) contains personality, and (7) includes beings that do moral thinking. Evolutionism has to violate the known fact of cause and effect to explain those observations—and cause and effect has never been violated.

Creationism complies completely with cause and effect. A God who is: (1) complex, (2) infinite, (3) eternal, (4) able to create, (5) a Designer with a purpose, (6) a Being with at least personality, and (7) a Being with at least morality would be an adequate cause of the universe we observe as an effect. As a matter of fact, the truth of cause and effect demands that we assume such a God exists.

2

Why Don't I Improve Faster?

"There he is."

"Hey!"

"How ya'll been?"

"You all right?"

"Good to see ya."

So went the chatter as five downtown Dallas businessmen gathered for their Friday brown bag lunch and Bible study group. Bill's office had become a sort of spiritual oasis for these men every week during their Friday lunch hour.

"Where's Bill?"

"I don't know."

"You'd think he could make it to his own office!"

"The receptionist said he left for lunch."

"Do you believe that guy? We've only been doing this for a couple of years now, and he forgets and goes *out* to lunch."

Just then the door opened. It was Bill. "I'll bet you thought I forgot," Bill said.

"Well, the thought had crossed our minds," Fred answered.

"You were right," Bill admitted. "I started thinking about Mexican food about an hour ago, and before I knew it I was on the elevator, headed out to get some. But I remembered just about the time I hit the street."

"We've all done the same thing," several of the other men admitted. After they had swapped a couple of embarrassing, forgotten appointment stories, Bill said, "You know what's *really* sad? I do the same thing with God."

"How do you mean?" Chuck asked.

"I seem to forget all about Him and go about my business—just as if He wasn't there," Bill answered. "Oh—if you ask me about depending on God, I'd probably answer all your questions right, but the point is, lots of times I just don't stop and think about Him. So I do things my way and end up disobeying God."

"You mean sinning," Chuck clarified.

"Well—yeah! And I feel guilty about it and don't have peace. Then it seems like God's a long way off."

"I know what you mean," Joe said. "I do that all the time. I end up with anxiety instead of peace. You think that's what keeps us from getting better faster?"

"It sure does with me," Bill concluded. "I end up feeling guilty about it, so I think about the problem—my sin—instead of the solution—becoming more like Christ."

"I've been doing some work on this area myself lately," Al answered. "I think if we just really believed, understood, and applied the payment Christ made for our sins on the cross we could grow better."

"Yeah. I *believe* that," Bill said. "But I don't experience it. Don't get me wrong—I think you're right. I didn't always believe that. When I found out Jesus Christ paid for all my sins—past, present, and future—I not only got saved, but I really felt free. But now I don't seem to feel as free as I did then."

The other men all admitted that they often felt more anxiety and guilt about their sin now than they did when they first believed. They decided to try to figure out why that was true.

"The problem may not be just in what we believe but in what we understand," Al suggested. "Do we really understand that God wants us to confess our sins to Him right away?"

"I know that in my head," Joe admitted, "but end up telling myself, 'God doesn't want to hear me confess that same old sin again.'"

"But He does," Al answered.

"I know," Joe continued, "but I don't always understand why God doesn't punish my sins."

"It's because He didn't forgive your *sins*," Al injected.

"Huh? God didn't forgive my sins?" Joe asked.

"No. He forgave *you* of your sins. Your sin wasn't forgiven; it was paid for and removed."

"I know all that," Bill insisted. "And I think I understand it, but I don't experience it. Somehow I don't seem to be applying what I believe and understand. I confess my sins all the time— well, most all the time, anyway—but I still feel an anxiety that keeps me from getting better. I believe and understand Jesus said I was supposed to experience peace, but sometimes I don't."

"Maybe we just need to realize that the struggle is normal," Pete suggested.

"It is?" Bill questioned.

"Exactly," Al added. "When we trust Christ for our salvation, we get a new nature. But we still have our old nature, and we always will have it—as long as we live in this body on earth. So becoming a Christian actually *begins* a battle between two natures inside us that wasn't there before. Inner peace comes as we realize daily that, even though we lose lots of battles, the war is already won."

"Oh—I see what you're getting at," Bill concluded. "That makes a big difference, if it's true. I feel weird because I'm experiencing an inward battle. But you're saying that's not weird; it's normal."

"Actually," Al added, "it's the best evidence that you're really saved and trying to get better. As a matter of fact, it's probably the best evidence that you actually *are* getting better. The more battles you win, the more useful you are to God, and the more there is for your old nature to attack. By concentrating on your sin with feelings of guilt and anxiety, you're really just feeding and strengthening that old nature. Peace in this life is peace in the midst of the struggle, knowing God has the victory won, instead of looking for a way to avoid the struggle."

ANXIETY AND THE PROBLEM OF GETTING BETTER

Let's break away from the group now and look at this issue a little closer. Here is an example that might help tune us in to the problem.

A middle-aged couple was discussing their financial security. The wife was concerned about the provisions her husband had made for the needs of the family in the case of his death. In order to relieve her anxious feelings, he explained to her that the investments that he had made in stocks and real estate would provide her and the family with an adequate income if he should die. But she continued to be anxious about the situation and did not experience the security he was talking about.

What would be some of the possible reasons for her continued anxiety? For one thing, she might not believe him. Then again, she might believe him but not understand the nature of the investments. Or third, she might not know how to apply the information. Those same three things can make us anxious as Christians and keep us from getting better faster.

Becoming a Christian does not always free people from their feelings of guilt, worry, and anxiety. But Jesus said, "Peace I leave with you; My peace I give to you; not as the world gives, do I give to you. Let not your heart be troubled, nor let it be fearful" (John 14:27). The Christian life, therefore, is designed to be free of anxiety and filled with peace.

But often it isn't! Christian psychiatrists, Christian psychologists, Christian counselors, and pastors are thronged by Christian patients unable to cope with their feelings of guilt and anxiety. Why? Possibly because the patients do not really believe what God has promised. Or they may believe it, but they do not understand all the implications of it. Or they may not know how to apply the benefits of their salvation to their lives on earth. I do not simply mean that they lack the facts necessary to know the message of salvation (although that is sometimes the case), but that the trust they placed in the Lord Jesus Christ at salvation has never, or only partially, become a reality in their everyday lives.

Those feelings of guilt and anxiety can cut off the strength we need to get better faster—at its source. The solutions may be the same three that the above-mentioned wife needed to solve her problem of anxiety—believing, understanding, and applying.

BELIEVING

We must believe God when He tells us that He paid for all the sin that causes our guilt feelings.

Paid in full. As our Lord died on the cross for the sins of the world, He said, "It is finished." The Greek word means "paid in full." The truth of the gospel, or good news, is that there is no sin left to feel guilty about. As the apostle Paul wrote, "God was in Christ reconciling the world to Himself, not counting their trespasses against them" (2 Corinthians 5:19).

All the sins of all time were paid for that day when God, having become the man Jesus of Nazareth, died in our place. All of Adam's sin, all of my sin, and all of the sin of my yet-to-be-conceived grandchildren (if Christ doesn't return before I have grandchildren) were paid for that day—now nearly two thousand years ago. Furthermore, when I received Christ, all that payment was applied to me, and God chose not only to forgive me but to forget my sins (Hebrews 8:12). Therefore, no Christian could ever have a position of guilt (a condemnation for an offense) before God for any sin—be it past, present, or future. The Bible says, "There is therefore now no condemnation for those who are in Christ Jesus" (Romans 8:1).

Natural sin. It is not merely a matter of God's paying for all our individual personally committed failures, but His paying for our sin nature. Our problem is not just one of having a record of sin but of having a nature of sin (Ephesians 4:18). Even if God wiped out our record of personal sin, we would continue to fail Him. We are not only sinners because we sin; we sin because we are sinners by nature. A dog is not a dog because he barks; he barks because he is a dog. If a dog never barked, he would be no less a dog. If we never committed a sin, we would be no less sinners.

I have heard people emphasize our need for Christ by saying, "There are two ways to get to heaven. One is never to commit any sins and the other is to receive Christ." But actually the first way is false. Even if we lived lives completely free from any sin (which, of course, no one except Jesus has), we would still be unfit for the presence of God because of our fallen sinful nature. When Christ died on the cross, He paid not only for our record of sins, but for our sin nature as well (Romans 6:1-7).

Understanding. Belief in God is essential for getting rid of that anxiety that can keep us from getting better spiritually. But believing is only helpful if we also have an *understanding* of the payment Christ made (Matthew 13:23). If we believe the work accomplished by Christ on the cross, but do not adequately understand it, we may never experience the peace available to us.

I believe Christ when He says I should have peace, Bill thought, *but why don't I experience it?*

Here are a few things we need to understand.

Conviction and confession. No Christian has ever been able to stop sinning. The apostle John, after about sixty years of ministry, told his Christian brothers and sisters, "If we say that we have no sin, we are deceiving ourselves, and the truth is not in us" (1 John 1:8).

We need to understand that God wants us to recognize our sin. Even though judgment for our sin is past and it is wiped off our record, it hinders our own personal growth and our fellowship with God. Children legitimately born into our families can never be guilty of being illegitimate. There is nothing they could do to not be our children. So it is when we are born into God's family. But it is also true that our children can be disobedient and grieve us deeply. In a similar way, our sin grieves God (Ephesians 4:30).

When we find ourselves sinning, God wants us to own up to it (see Psalm 32:3-4; Psalm 51). The Bible says, "If we confess our sins, He is faithful and righteous to forgive us our sins and to cleanse us from all unrighteousness" (1 John 1:9). The word here translated "confess" means "to agree with." God wants us to agree with Him that our sin is as wrong as He says it is.

That brings up an interesting question. What failures should we mention to God? Obviously I sin much more than I am aware of. Furthermore, I forget to confess things I am aware of. The answer? Confess the sin the Holy Spirit of God has brought to your attention.

Every one of us is in a different place in his spiritual development. Although all believers are being convicted by the same Holy Spirit (John 16:8; Romans 8:14-15), He is not dealing with the same problems in all of us. He may be convicting me of my lack of patience. You may not have a problem with patience. Or God may be convicting you of something He wants you to recognize first. As time goes on and we yield ourselves to God, He continually convicts us of more and more of those sinful areas of our lives.

Having been a Christian for over twenty years now, I often feel I am more sinful than I was twenty years ago. But even that is comforting—knowing God is working on me. The fact is, I am convicted by the Holy Spirit of many more of my sins than I was twenty years ago.

Sin is not just *forgiven*—it's *paid for*. "Just a semantic difference," you say? Not necessarily! The modern liberal humanists also say that sins are forgiven. But what *they* mean is that sins are essentially overlooked. If God could have overlooked sin, there would have been no need for Christ to die. He would then be accepting sin and therefore would not be a holy and righteous God. In that case we would have no hope in the universe—no sinless perfect Holy One to come to. But since God is holy and righteous and perfect by nature, He could not merely forgive sin.

It had to be paid for. So He paid for it Himself. God the Son became man, took all our sins upon Himself, and died in our place.

But now that sin has been paid for, *people* can be forgiven of their sins. People can be accepted. This idea is reflected in the Lord's Prayer in which Christ instructs us to pray, "And forgive us our debts" (Matthew 6:12). He does not suggest that we ask forgiveness for *our debts*, but that we pray "forgive *us* our debts." In his letter to the Colossians, Paul reminds them, "The Lord forgave *you*" (Colossians 3:13, italics added). It was the Colossian believers, not just their sins, who were forgiven.

If God were in the business of forgiving each sin as we confessed it, then it would be reasonable to assume that newly committed sins had yet to be forgiven. We would have to take each one of them to God in some way to get them forgiven. Since no one could possibly remember all his sins or be sure he was sorry enough or sincere enough, or whatever, then he could never be sure he had met the requirements to get them forgiven.

The anxiety of that guilt is hard to avoid. Paul does not list specific sins for God to forgive. Instead he asks, "Who will set *me* free from the body of this death?" Then he answers his own question by exclaiming, "Thanks be to God through Jesus Christ our Lord!" (Romans 7:24-25, italics added). *We* have been set free because all our sins are paid for. We are forgiven, so anxiety is unnecessary.

APPLYING

Anxiety that prevents growth may be caused by our failure to believe God when He tells us Christ paid for our sin completely. Then again, we may believe it but not understand it. There is yet a third possibility—we may not know how to apply that truth to our lives each day. Here are a few thoughts that may help in application.

The warfare within. As Christians, we have a new nature inside us. We are new creatures in Christ (2 Corinthians 5:17). But as long as we have to live in this present earthly body, we will also have our same old sin nature. Those two natures will constantly be at war with each other (Romans 7:15-25; Galatians 5:17). When our old nature wins a battle and we sin, God tells us to confess it and go on feeding and developing our new nature. But sometimes we hesitate to confess it, thinking, "Oh, I can't bring that sin to God *again!*" Or when we confess it, we refuse to believe God's promise that it has been paid for. We may even (consciously or subconsciously) try to punish ourselves. Then anxiety sets in, serving only to feed and strengthen that old sin nature.

Losing battles but winning the war. The peaceful Christian life comes not from winning all the battles with our old nature. It comes from realizing that those battles are normal, not unusual. They are not weird struggles that only a few "backsliders" experience; they are standard operating procedure for the believer (1 Corinthians 10:13).

Furthermore, there is no way out of the battles. We live in an age when Christians seem to think struggles should be eliminated. Not so! The new nature within us is up against powerful odds. We do not have to look for a struggle; the struggle is there naturally as we strive to live righteously in Satan's unrighteous world system.

Picture yourself inside a football stadium, trying to get out, just before the crowd is let in to see the Superbowl. As the gates are opened, you have to struggle to get out, simply because everybody else is pushing to get in. The spiritual life is like that. Struggles against our old nature will be difficult, and failures— even losses—are normal. We may even be tempted at times to stop trying to be righteous. But God wants us to "press on," even as Paul did (Philippians 3:12).

Even though we may lose lots of battles, we have a sure word from God that the war is already won. Our sin nature is like a killer on death row. It is not dead yet, but someday it will be. As long as we must live in this physical body, our sin nature is still alive and well. But it has been judged dead and condemned. When we are delivered from this body, it will be gone forever.

Even though we may lose battles every day, the victory is sure. The sin is paid for, and we can confess it to God, knowing our forgiveness is already accomplished. Peace in the Christian life lies not in freedom from turmoil, but in confidence in God's promise of ultimate victory.

I once heard of a rich man who called two artists to his house because he wanted a large painting for a certain empty wall. He told them he wanted them to paint a water scene depicting peace, and he would buy the one picture best communicating true peace. One artist painted a quiet lake in the middle of a forest. The second artist painted a boiling waterfall full of jagged rocks, with a bird sitting on a nest built on a strong tree limb overhanging the falls. The rich man bought the second painting. Unlike the first painting, the peace did not depend on the circumstances.

In the spiritual struggle Christians go through every day, peace lies not in avoiding the struggle, but in the confidence that we are sitting firmly in God's hand—in the midst of the turmoil.

Lots of things can keep us from getting better faster. The purpose of this chapter is not to examine *all* of those things, but only one—anxiety. Anxiety, too, may have many causes, but a crucial one is our failure to believe, understand, and apply the work of Christ. We tend to forget what Christ accomplished at the cross. The point of this chapter is to say that this is one of the most important truths in our lives—even *after* we become Christians. A basic part—maybe the most crucial part—of our Christian growth depends on getting rid of the anxiety caused by guilt. Simply put, a major part of that is accomplished when we saturate our minds every day with the remembrance of what Christ accomplished on the cross.

3
What If I Don't Like to Witness?

"Roger, seven-two-seven. Clear to one-one-thousand. Contact Denver approach control one-two-five-point-eight."

Although the pilot heard the transmission, his mind was tuned to a more personal matter. Would he make it to Denver in time to catch his flight home to Dallas—as a passenger? Steve had been an airline captain for ten years now. He knew all sorts of ways to speed things up a bit without sacrificing safety. But this time he only had five minutes between landing this plane and taking off in the one he wanted to ride home to Dallas.

He picked up the microphone and responded. "Seven-two-seven, proceeding to one-one-thousand, switching to Denver on one-two-five-point-eight. Good-day."

"Good-day," came the reply from the controller.

"Let's keep her clean as long as we can," Steve said to his copilot. (That meant not to use wing flaps and extensions until absolutely necessary, because they would slow down the aircraft.)

It was the end of a long flight from Miami to Dallas to Colorado Springs, and now the one last little hop to Denver—then home to his family.

He made it. Just made it. Three hundred and sixty miles per hour descent. One hundred-sixty miles per hour landing speed on runway two-six (which was crucial, since that runway got them to the gate the quickest. Then came the dash out of the cockpit, down to the next gate, and onto the plane.

As the plane began its "push-back" away from the gatehouse, Steve was pushing his way past the flight attendants. He apologized to every third person or so as he bumped into people with his flight bag and suitcase. He finally managed to pack himself into the last seat left on the airplane—the middle seat in the last row.

By the time he finally got his long legs and his two bags squeezed in, Steve was already well-introduced to the men he sat between. They were both huge guys, and Steve himself was six-foot-two. But they finally settled back and watched the take-off of their one and a half hour flight to Dallas.

The man in the window seat seemed quiet and unfriendly, so Steve turned to the man in the aisle seat. After learning his name was Ken, he said, "What do *you* do for a living?" It was obvious what Steve did. His airline captain's uniform announced it loud and clear.

"I sell textiles to large retail stores," Ken answered.

"Do you enjoy it?" Steve probed.

"Yeah," Ken responded hesitantly. "But the economy seems to have affected buying quite a bit."

They continued to chat, but both men had a hidden agenda. Both were Christians and believed they ought to witness to each other. Finally, in the midst of a discussion about inflation, Ken blurted out, "By the way, Steve, are you a Christian?"

Steve was shocked by the question, even though he had been trying to figure out a way to ask Ken the same thing. "Yes, as a matter of fact, I am," he answered.

Ken, realizing that even an unbeliever might say that, pursued with, "Can you point to a time when you trusted Jesus Christ personally for your sins?"

"Yes, but wait a minute," Steve returned. "I've been sitting here trying to figure out a way to ask you the same thing."

"Really!" Now Ken was convinced—and a bit embarrassed. After they had chuckled a bit over the fact that they were both Christians trying to figure out how to witness to each other, Ken said, "Tell me, Steve, don't you feel a little uneasy about witnessing to people you don't know?"

"Sure do. To tell you the truth, I hate it," Steve answered.

"But don't you feel like it's your duty as a Christian to confront everyone you see with the gospel? I really get to feeling guilty about it. I wouldn't want anyone to miss heaven because *I* didn't tell them how to get saved."

"I think it's a matter of wisdom," Steve replied. "In Colossians four five the apostle Paul said, 'Conduct yourselves with wisdom toward outsiders, making the most of the opportunity.' So it seems like making the most of the opportunity involves doing whatever is the wisest thing to do. I have found that a relational type of evangelism is wiser in many cases than a confrontation."

"You mean forming a friendship with an unbeliever and letting him come to Christ as he is ready?" Ken questioned.

"Uh-huh! I believe I'm doing evangelism when I'm helping my unbelieving neighbor start his car or just having him and his wife over to watch a football game on TV."

"I've heard about that," Ken continued, "but do you really think that's the way they did it in the Bible?"

"I think so," Steve answered. "Nobody does evangelism *exactly* the way it was done in the Bible, but Jesus Christ spent lots of time with sinners. His apostles were basically trained through relationships with Him. Paul seems to have made friends with the people he reached with the gospel. Many of his letters end with names of people he was close to personally. He even told the Thessalonians he had a fond affection for them."

"But does it work?" Ken interrupted. "Most of the statistics I hear about people coming to Christ are from Christians who use some kind of confrontational program or system."

"I think there is a real place for confrontational evangelism. But," Steve pointed out, "that doesn't mean it is always the best approach with everybody. Some people are turned off or offended by that. And if you look at the long-term picture, those unbelievers who come to Christ through a relationship with some Christian are more apt to continue on as part of some regular Christian fellowship."

"Follow-up does seem to be a problem," Ken admitted.

"But," Steve persisted, "when the person who comes to Christ is your friend, follow-up is sort of built-in—it's just more of that same friendship."

Let's break away from their discussion and consider more closely this alternative to the traditional confrontational approach to evangelism.

RELATIONAL EVANGELISM

I heard an interesting variation to the old story of the boy who cried, "Wolf." It goes like this:

Once upon a time a group of villagers instructed their young shepherd: "When you see a wolf, cry, 'Wolf,' and we'll come with guns and pitchforks."

The next day the boy was tending his sheep when he saw a lion in the distance. He cried out: "Lion, lion!" But no one came. The lion killed several sheep. The shepherd boy was distressed. "Why didn't you come when I yelled?" he asked.

"There are no lions in this part of the country," an older man replied. "It is *wolves* we are afraid of."

The young shepherd learned a valuable lesson from the experience. *People respond only to what they are prepared to believe.*

A crucial question must be answered as we consider the subject of communicating the gospel: What is the unbeliever *prepared* to believe? Possibly a more important question than "How do we lead people to Christ?" might be "How do we prepare people to understand the gospel?" Whether we attempt to have people raise their hands, walk down an aisle, read through a booklet, check the appropriate box on a card, or make a decision at a crusade is not the most crucial issue. The long-term results of our evangelistic efforts will depend on how we have *prepared* unbelievers to make that essential decision.

WHAT IS THE DIFFERENCE BETWEEN RELATIONAL AND CONFRONTATIONAL EVANGELISM?

Most of the instruction for witnessing given to Christians in recent years has been for confrontational evangelism. In other words, the focal point is on the decision the unbeliever must make. Possibly this results from our Western mentality, which emphasizes a product rather than a process, a decision rather than a way of thinking. The Eastern mindset, however, is much more process-oriented. (We must remember that God chose to write the Bible and, at the start at least, communicate the truths revealed in the Bible through the Eastern mentality.) That is not to say that a confrontation or decision is not essential. A decision to receive Christ is as essential to a relational approach as it is to a confrontational approach to evangelism. The difference is one of emphasis.

In relational evangelism the emphasis is on a relationship established between the believer and the unbeliever. Here the decision to receive Christ is a natural outgrowth of the process of the development of that relationship. In confrontational evangelism, the emphasis is placed on some method used to guide an unbeliever to that decision itself. Relational evangelism focuses in on the process that prepares a person to understand the gospel so that he can make a rational decision.

A twelve-year-old boy had just completed a swimming course at the local pool. A pal asked him, "What's the best way to teach a girl to swim?"

"First, you put your arm around her waist, then you take her left hand—" he began to explain seriously.

"She's my sister," the boy interrupted.

"Oh," grunted the twelve-year-old, "push her off the edge."

The evangelical community is often guilty of inconsistency in the way it deals with people. Like the twelve-year-old, we often practice a put-your-arm-around-her-waist attitude among Christians and a push-her-off-the-edge attitude toward evangelism. A relationship approach to evangelism suggests that we extend the put-your-arm-around-her-waist mentality to evangelism. Friendship evangelism, however, to a relationalist does not simply mean being friendly while doing confrontational evangelism. Instead it encompasses the whole attitude toward missionary activity.

IS THERE A BIBLICAL BASIS FOR RELATIONAL EVANGELISM?

God used a multitude of different ways to communicate Himself to man. He revealed Himself through nature (Romans 1:18-20), miracles (John 2:11), and the Scriptures (2 Peter 1:20-21). We must observe, however, that God did not consider His communication concerning Himself complete until He became a man and lived with us (John 1:14) and established relationships with us "while we were yet sinners" (Romans 5:8). As a matter of fact, that was so central to God the Son's incarnational activity that He gained the reputation of being "a gluttonous man, and a drunkard, a friend of tax gatherers and sinners" (Luke 7:34). If God's only purpose in sending Christ was to pay for our sins, He could have done that in three days. Instead, He took over thirty years to grow up among us and live out relationships with us. If Christ is indeed our example, then spending time establishing relationships with unbelievers is a must.

Not only did our Lord Jesus Christ form relationships with people, but God used many other relationships to communicate Himself. The Bible is filled with examples of people who communicated godliness through relationships. God has chosen to reveal Himself by bringing one person up alongside another in such a way that the one can become infected with the glory of God as it radiates from the other. There were Elijah and Elisha (1 Kings 19:19-21); Eli and Samuel (1 Samuel 3:1-19); Moses and Joshua (Deuteronomy 3:12); Naomi and Ruth (Ruth 1:15-18); Mary and Elizabeth (Luke 1:39-45); Christ and the twelve—especially Peter (John 21:15); Luke and Theophilus (Luke 1:1-4 and Acts 1:1-2); Peter and John Mark (1 Peter 5:13); and many others.[1]

The teachings of the apostle Paul also include the importance of relationships with unbelievers. When he told Timothy to entrust the things he had taught him to others (2 Timothy 2:2), he spent only a little time telling Timothy *how* to go about it. The reason?

---

1. David A. DeWitt, *Answering the Tough Ones* (Chicago: Moody, 1980), p. 34.

Timothy knew very well how Paul did that. He told Timothy, "The Lord's bondservant must *not be quarrelsome*, but be *kind* to all, able to teach, *patient* when wronged, with *gentleness* correcting those who are in opposition, if perhaps God may grant them repentance leading to the knowledge of the truth . . ." (2 Timothy 2:24-25, italics added).

Paul demonstrated the importance of relationships by his life-style. After leaving Thessalonica he wrote back to the church, saying "We proved to be gentle among you, as a nursing mother tenderly cares for her own children. Having thus a fond affection for you, we were well-pleased to impart to you not only the gospel of God but also our own lives, because you had become very dear to us" (1 Thessalonians 2:7-8).

Paul was upset with the Corinthians when they began disassociating themselves from friendships with unbelievers. This was to be the heart of their evangelistic outreach. He assured them that they were not to shy away from relationships with people of the world (1 Corinthians 5:9-12). Paul chose to follow Christ's example of relating to people by living among them. He communicated the gospel through many and various means (1 Corinthians 9:22). One crucial means was the development of strong, close, communicative relationships.

Peter had trouble with this idea of establishing relationships with unbelievers—especially Gentiles. So God gave Peter an illustration; God was redeeming a people for Himself, and anyone could be saved. He called Peter to Caesarea to meet a Gentile named Cornelius, who had gathered a group of potential believers. The striking thing about that group was that they were Cornelius's "relatives and close friends" (Acts 10:24). Cornelius used his existing relationships with those "friends" ultimately to bring them to Christ. God wanted Peter to see what the Holy Spirit was doing.

I have also been asked, "Doesn't the book of Acts teach confrontational instead of relational evangelism?" We need to notice that the book of Acts is transitional; the events in the beginning of the book are different from those at the end of it.

The changes include methods of evangelism. People did not continue to have tongues of fire over their heads as a prelude to their preaching. Toward the end of the book miracles and healings were not always available to bring attention to the gospel, nor were thousands added to the church every day.

It is important to notice that the emphasis changed from confronting the masses to relating to individuals. The early part of the book of Acts sees regular reference to the numbers of people being added to the church with little record of the personalities of the individuals involved. We read that they added three thousand to their number (Acts 2:41). We see "multitudes of men and women" (Acts 5:14) added in Jerusalem. We find Philip addressing "multitudes" in Samaria (Acts 8:6). We observe "considerable numbers" believing in Antioch (Acts 11:21, 26) and "crowds" being addressed in Galatia (Acts 13:45; 14:1).

But as we continue on in the book of Acts, the emphasis on the numbers, multitudes, and crowds decreases, as smaller groups and individuals are given more attention. Notice in the following list how the attention given to individuals is seldom and far between in the early part of the book and more regular during the later part:

- Philip with Simon the sorcerer—Acts 8:13
- Philip with the Ethiopian eunuch—Acts 8:39
- Peter with Cornelius—Acts 10:22
- Paul with Sergius Paulus—Acts 13:7, 12
- The lame man at Lystra—Acts 14:8
- Lydia from Thyatira—Acts 16:14
- The "slave girl"—Acts 16:16
- The Philippian jailer—Acts 16:31
- Jason—Acts 17:17
- Crispus—Acts 18:8
- Apollos—Acts 18:24
- Demetrius the silversmith—Acts 19:24
- The boy who fell—Acts 20:12

- All the individuals involved in Paul's arrest and imprisonment
  — Acts 20:27

In applying this transition, we need to be cautious not to strictly eliminate either emphasis. The question is, What are the cultural conditions of the society in which we are witnessing? If the people have never heard the gospel message and (as in the first part of Acts) basic information is needed, then confrontational or mass evangelism is probably going to be most effective. As Christian ideas become more known, a more relational approach of making friends will probably be most effective.

The emphasis in Acts, then, changes from confrontational to relational. The graph would be something like this:

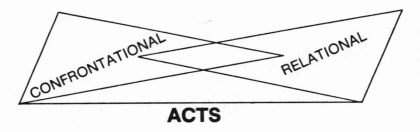

ACTS

IS THERE ANY PRACTICAL ADVANTAGE TO RELATIONAL EVANGELISM?

It is entirely possible that our friends or potential friends are the greatest untapped source of unbelievers available. Two things are true of most people: one, they need friends, and two, they have very few of them, if any. Alan Loy McGinnis, in his book *The Friendship Factor*, estimates that only ten percent of all Americans have close friends. He writes:

> Some of America's leading psychologists and therapists were asked how many men ever have real friends. The bleak replies were "not nearly enough" and "too few." Most guessed at 10%. Richard Farson, professor at the Humanistic Psychology Institute in San

Francisco, says, "Millions of people in America have never had one minute in their whole lifetime where they could 'let down' and share with another person their deeper feelings."[2]

The unbelievers in our neighborhoods, offices, factories, schools, and other places life takes us everyday, need friendships. If we were to write down the name of everyone we came in contact with all day long, then cross out the ones we feel sure are Christians, we would have a tremendous list of the best resources for evangelism.

Wayne McDill, in his book *Making Friends for Christ,* estimates that we each have about twelve such vital unbeliever contacts. He reports:

In my own research I have asked Christians in personal evangelism seminars to write, in five minutes, the names of the people they know who meet the following tests: (1) their acquaintance is on a first-name basis; (2) these people live in the ministry area of the church; (3) they give no evidence of being Christian. The results have been very consistent. A small group of 23 seminar participants named 263 people. A larger group of 77 named 982 people. All the totals together indicate that each seminar participant averages knowing about 12 people who meet these three criteria. What a tremendous potential for evangelism this can be if we will learn how to make the most of these relationships.[3]

Is there a practical advantage for the local church? All the research seems to indicate that the vast majority of those who come to Christ and continue on to be a regular part of a local church come through close friends and relatives already in that church. Repeated evaluation of evangelistic crusades and programs used by churches will show that those who stick around

2. Alan Loy McGinnis, *The Friendship Factor* (Minneapolis: Augsburg, 1979), p. 11.
3. Wayne McDill, *Making Friends for Christ* (Nashville: Broadman, 1979), p. 29.

after they make the decision are generally those who have already established relationships with someone in the church.

Win Arn of the Institute for American Church Growth polled a number of people in a variety of churches, asking each why he joined a particular church. Arn reports: "Walk-ins account for approximately 4 to 6% of a total congregation. Programs bring in 2 to 4%. The pastor is listed by 4 to 7% as being the major reason they are in their church. A special need: 2 to 4%. Visitation: 1 to 2%. Sunday school: 4 to 6%. City-wide mass evangelistic crusades: .001%. Friends and/or relatives: 70 to 90%."[4]

WHY DOES FOLLOW-UP SEEM TO BE A PROBLEM IN MOST EVANGELISTIC EFFORTS?

Recently I saw a cartoon of a middle-aged man who had just returned from jogging. "How far did you run?" his wife asked.

"Five miles," he replied.

"Five miles!" she exclaimed. "How in the world could you have run five miles? You've only been gone ten minutes!"

He answered, "I found a short-cut!"

Many of the problems we find in follow-up may result from trying to find a short-cut to evangelism.

First of all, we must face the fact that follow-up is generally a problem to any confrontational style of evangelism. My own personal (admittedly unscientific) survey of people involved in a confrontational style of evangelism shows that in general only 4% to 15% of the people who indicate that they have made a decision actually continue on in Christianity for any prolonged period of time. The highest percentages I have ever been able to obtain are around 25%, and those are exceedingly rare.

Why is follow-up so difficult? I'd like to suggest it's because of the way the evangelism was done. From time to time I have done my own research with people doing friendship or relational

4. Win Arn, "People Are Asking," *Church Growth: America*, March-April 1979 (Pasadena, Calif.: Institute for American Church Growth), p. 11.

evangelism. Invariably I find that over 80 percent (and often over 90 percent) of those who came to Christ through a relational approach continue on as a regular part of some Christian fellowship. The reason is not that the follow-up material was better, nor that the discipleship program or people were superior. The difference was in the way they came to Christ in the first place. When people trust Christ in the midst of a long-established relationship with a neighbor, friend, or relative, they tend to continue getting fed through that same relationship.

After years of evangelism and frustration over the lack of follow-up, Wayne McDill writes: "It became increasingly apparent to me that we had created the follow-up problem for ourselves through our very approach to evangelism."[5] He goes on to conclude: "Evangelism will be effective toward making disciples in direct proportion to its dependence on the establishment and cultivation of meaningful relationships."[6]

Jesus beckoned the disciples to "follow Me." He called to Levi while he was still in his tax office (Luke 5:27). It appears that Jesus had more of a follow-Me program than a follow-up program. Even that wasn't a program; it was a relational life-style. Pre-evangelism, evangelism, and follow-up were hard to distinguish with Christ. He asked unbelieving sinners to follow Him. After His resurrection and ascension, those who did gave their lives to start His church. Somewhere en route they crossed over that line and became believers. But the exact point of their decision—though definite—is hard to find.

When would confrontational evangelism be most effective? Probably when we are dealing with people who have not already been vaccinated with enough Christian terms and religious ideas to keep them from getting the real disease. Practically, this would be in segments of the world's population that have not already heard about Christianity. The largest such segment would be children—whose unconscious mental computers are not

5. McDill, p. 6.
6. Ibid.

already filled with things that reject the gospel because of previous experience.

Confrontationalism has a place in evangelism. Nevertheless, if we are to reach adults (and New Testament evangelism certainly did not exclude the adults) in a society cluttered with religious works, we need to give serious consideration to the concept of relational evangelism.

4

Are There Any Mistakes in the Bible?

Mike's arms strained as he turned the huge steering wheel. *Sure wish they'd get power steering on these things*, he thought to himself. As his big city bus rounded the corner from Lamar Street to Commerce, the night lights of downtown Dallas sprinkled the darkness with an array of colors.

He felt tense. As he pulled to a stop at the red light, he looked at his big, railroad-style pocket watch. Twelve thirty-one A.M. —he was right on schedule. If the supervisor got the message, he should be waiting for him at the next intersection.

Sure enough. That familiar white shirt and black hat stood out to Mike like an extra stoplight. A bus driver did not always welcome a visit from his supervisor, but this time was different.

"Howdy, Mike." The supervisor smiled as he climbed in and took the seat behind his driver. "Hear you've got a little problem."

"Well, Mr. Briggs, I'm not sure what to do about my ol' buddy back there." Mike pointed his thumb over his shoulder as he kept the bus moving down Commerce Street. In the third seat from the rear of the bus sat a scruffy-looking man in his early sixties, leaning up against the wall. "He's been on here for over two hours, now," Mike continued. "He's ridden around the whole route three times, weaving back and forth in his seat. Now I think he's passed out."

"I'll go have a look," said Briggs.

After several unsuccessful attempts to communicate with the man, they notified the police, who came and escorted him off the bus.

Then the bus was empty. Only Mike and his supervisor were left to ride the hollow coach back to the station.

"Mind if I see what you're reading?" Mr. Briggs asked, noticing the top of a paperback sticking out of Mike's supply box.

"Help yourself," Mike encouraged, as he wheeled the bus through the dark streets.

"Oh! It's about the accuracy of the Bible," Mr. Briggs exclaimed, thumbing through the book. Then he added, "Are you a Christian, Mike?"

"Yes, sir," Mike responded.

"How about that? I am, too," Briggs returned.

That inspired one of those unique, exciting conversations where Christian brotherhood takes precedence over any employer/employee relationship.

After a few minutes Mr. Briggs asked, "You've done a lot of reading about the accuracy of the Bible, have you?"

"Well—yeah. As a matter of fact, I have, lately," Mike confessed.

"Then I'd like to ask you something," Mr. Briggs pursued. "A Christian friend of mine says arguing about whether or not there are errors in the Bible just causes divisions in the church, when what we really need is to be united. What do *you* think?"

Mike had stopped the bus at one of those extra long red lights, so he was able to turn toward Briggs as he answered. "Oh, I guess *arguing* never does any good," he began. "But as far as this being a subject that causes divisions, I really don't see *that* as a good reason to avoid it. Ya know, any crucial issue causes divisions. And it seems to me like this *is* a crucial issue. Think about it. If the words of the Bible could have some errors in them, then how in the world could we ever be sure of what God wants us to know?"

"But isn't that making the Bible more important than Christ?" Briggs asked.

The light turned green, and Mike began rolling again as he answered. "It's not either/or; it's both/and. When you get right down to it, the only way you can know what Christ said is through the Bible. If that's got mistakes in it, there's no way at all to know Christ for sure."

"I guess that's right," Mr. Briggs admitted. "But then why don't they teach that in my church?"

"I'd say that most people in your church do believe that. And, well, I don't know your friend," Mike continued hesitantly, "but the books I've been reading lately say that many people don't teach that because they really aren't sure the Bible is right anymore. Lots of seminaries have some liberal teachers who don't believe the Bible is completely accurate. Fact is, it rubs off on a lot of Christians."

"But aren't there really a lot of mistakes in the Bible?" Briggs persisted.

"Do you know of any?" Mike asked, snatching a glance at his supervisor.

"No. Not right off," Mr. Briggs admitted. "But surely there are some, or those liberal scholars wouldn't be saying so."

"I'm not so sure," Mike added. "There are also lots of scholars who have investigated the so-called mistakes and don't think they're mistakes at all. I wonder if those liberal critics have ever really looked at those 'mistakes' to see if there are good explanations for them."

"Well, maybe not," Mr. Briggs commented. "But I think I'll leave it up to the scholars to wrestle it out."

"I wouldn't do that, if I were you," Mike added.

"Why not?"

"Don't you think it's important for you as well as the scholars to make Christ the Lord of your life?"

"Sure!" Briggs responded.

"It seems to me you'll have trouble doing that if you're not sure about the accuracy of the Bible. How else are you gonna know how to follow Christ?"

THE ACCURACY OF THE BIBLE

Let's get off the bus at this stop and think through some of the points Mike was able to discuss with his supervisor.

The discussion surfaced five crucial questions about the subject of possible errors in the Bible. Here is a closer look at those issues.

IS THIS SUBJECT DIVISIVE?

Sure is!

Any subject that takes a stand on any crucial issue is divisive when it attempts to give an answer. Christianity itself is divisive. The nature of God is divisive. Salvation is divisive. The person of Jesus Christ is divisive. As a matter of fact, we will generally find more tension in our conversations about Jesus Christ than about Buddha, Mohammed, or any other religious figure. Why? Because He claims to have a sure and certain answer.

The world is hurting for an answer, and Christians cannot avoid those subjects simply because they are divisive. Christians are no more free to keep Christ's answers to themselves than a doctor would be to keep the knowledge of a preventive vaccination to himself, just because some people might be against it.

Truth always makes a division with error. And that is exactly what we are talking about—truth, answers. If the Bible is not a record of God's revelation to man, recorded in the writings of the original authors without any errors whatsoever, then we have no certain truth—no answers. If only parts of the Bible are true, and parts contain errors, as some suppose, then how do we determine which parts are right?

The "how," of course, is that we decide based on our human evaluations. But human evaluations are always a mixture. Sometimes we are right, and sometimes we are wrong. When we use our opinions to decide which parts of the Bible are true, we reduce a solid answer to one mixed with some truth and some errors. *People* then become the standard. Our own thoughts and feelings become the god of our values. That's humanism. Humanism soothes the pain of divisiveness; everybody just believes what seems best for himself.

Whereas *people* are sometimes right and sometimes wrong,

the Bible is never wrong. There are no demonstrable errors in the Bible, even though it leaves itself wide open for investigation by listing all kinds of dates, places, people, and events that can be checked out archaeologically and historically.

The idea of a completely inerrant Bible is going to cause divisions. It can't be helped—not if we are going to have any answers beyond our hurting selves to give a hurting world.

IF WE INSIST THERE ARE NO ERRORS IN THE BIBLE, ARE WE MAKING THE BIBLE MORE IMPORTANT THAN CHRIST?

To this question I would like to ask, "Christ who?"

Are we asking people to believe in some "Christ" idea that we made up in our own minds? Is He (or It) some mirage Christians have conjured up to impose on ourselves and the rest of the world? If that is the case, we really do not have any right to tell anybody about it at all. We had better return to our own private religiosity and keep quiet.

"Oh, but," you say, "there really was a Jesus of Nazareth who physically existed, walked the earth, died for our sins, and rose from the dead, demonstrating that His message was real and truly from God."

Of course there was. But how do we know that He really paid for our sins on the cross? How do we know what kind of life He wants us to live?

The Bible tells us so—that's how! True, there are non-Christian historians like Josephus who wrote of the life, miracles, death, and resurrection of Jesus of Nazareth. But nothing beyond that is possible without a conviction that the Bible contains the truth about that Jesus without any errors.

Some have decided to follow the general teachings of Jesus in the Bible, yet they continue to believe that some of those are recorded with errors. Such folks have to discard a lot of the Bible's record of Him. Why? Because He constantly revealed His own belief that the books of the Bible written before His time were without error.

The Lord Jesus Christ quoted the Old Testament in about 10

percent of everything that He said.[1] His response to Satan's temptations was to declare that human life was to be lived based on "EVERY WORD THAT PROCEEDS OUT OF THE MOUTH OF GOD" (Matthew 4:4; cf. Deuteronomy 8:3). Jesus didn't teach us to live by the general basic concepts of the Bible, but by "every word" of it.

He went on to say, "Not the smallest letter or stroke shall pass away from the Law, until all is accomplished" (Matthew 5:18). According to Christ, the law (the Bible) is true, down to its very words, letters, and even the strokes that make up the pieces of the letters.

Later, when quoting what Moses wrote in the book of Exodus, our Lord preceded His quote by saying, "For God said" (Matthew 15:4). Jesus taught that every word and letter in the Scriptures was completely free of error. When human authors (like Moses) wrote the Bible, it was what "God said," not just what "Moses said."

Not only did the Lord Jesus Christ believe that the Old Testament Scripture "cannot be broken" (John 10:35), but He also saw a future volume of literature (the New Testament), which would be recorded under the authority of the apostles. That New Testament would contain His own words. In Luke 6:46, He declares, "And why do you call Me, 'Lord, Lord,' and do not do what I say?" Obviously what He said would have to be recorded without error if we are going to know what to "do."

How would the New Testament be written? Jesus explained to the apostles, "When He, the Spirit of truth, comes, He will guide you into all the truth; for He will not speak on His own initiative, but whatever He hears, He will speak; and He will disclose to you what is to come. He shall glorify Me; for He shall take of Mine, and shall disclose it to you" (John 16:13-14). That New Testament revelation was written by those apostles and a few others (John Mark, Luke, Jesus' half brothers James and Jude,

---

1. Harry Rimmer, *Internal Evidence of Inspiration* (Grand Rapids: Eerdmans, 1938), p. 227.

plus the author of Hebrews), whose authority was sanctioned by the apostles.

The New Testament was written under the apostles' authority from the mid-forties A.D. to the mid-nineties A.D. Then the Lord Jesus Christ revealed the last book of the Bible to the apostle John—the book of Revelation—in about A.D. 96. But He ended the book of Revelation by saying, "I, Jesus, have sent My angel to testify to you these things . . . I testify to everyone who hears the words of the prophecy of this book: if anyone adds to them, God shall add to him the plagues which are written in this book; and if anyone takes away from the words of the book of this prophecy, God shall take away his part from the tree of life and from the holy city, which are written in this book" (Revelation 22:16*a*, 18-19).

If we wish to put Jesus Christ first, then we must also accept His view of the Bible. That view seems to include an Old Testament and a New Testament of written revelation, "every word" without any error of any kind, and that written revelation was to end with the book of Revelation—the last book written by the apostle John about A.D. 96.

WHY DON'T WE HEAR THIS IN CHURCH?

We *do* hear it in many churches.

People want to hear the Bible preached as truth that they can use to guide them through the coming week. So why aren't many pastors preaching the answers that the Bible has to offer? They simply are not sure the Bible has the right answers anymore.

James Montgomery Boice has written a booklet called *Does Inerrancy Matter?* He addressed this aspect of the subject as well as anyone, so let's consider his words carefully. Boice writes:

> A . . . reason why inerrancy is important is *preaching*. There are many eloquent preachers today, but not many who do expository preaching. So the sermons are man centered, weak and shallow—and most Christians know it. Sometimes they are kind in their evaluation: "I guess I just didn't get much out of the sermon this

morning." Sometimes they are more critical: "Why doesn't my minister preach the Bible?" Behind each of these comments is the sense that something is wrong. Many preachers talk about the Bible. They say they believe it. But they do not really teach it. Why is this? The reason (whether the ministers or the seminaries in which they are trained admit it or not) is that the majority of today's preachers are no longer sure that the Lord has spoken in Scripture. . . .

Recently, Western Reserve University mailed a questionnaire to 10,000 clergymen in five major US denominations. It received a reply from 7,442 of them. On it was this question: "Do you believe the Bible to be the inspired Word of God?" This was weaker than asking: "Do you believe in an inerrant Bible?" or, "Do you believe in verbal inspiration?" since there are all kinds of views of inspiration, not all of which concern the actual words of Scripture. Some views seem to suggest only that the writers were filled with some special religious insight. All the question was really asking was: Do you believe the Bible is God's Word in any unusual sense? Yet in spite of the level at which the question was asked,

  82% of the Methodists
  89% of the Episcopalians
  81% of the United Presbyterians
  57% of the Baptists
  57% of the Lutherans
answered, "NO!"[2]

When so many of the Christian leaders surveyed do not believe the Bible is God's Word, it is little wonder people are looking elsewhere for the answers to life's problems.

AREN'T THERE ERRORS IN THE BIBLE?

The point I have been making is that the Bible is 100 percent accurate, 100 percent of the time. That sort of claim generally initiates the following kinds of questions.

What about scientifically inaccurate statements? When I say that there are no errors in the Bible I am often asked something

2. James Montgomery Boice, *Does Inerrancy Matter?* (International Council on Biblical Inerrancy, 1979), pp. 18-19.

like, "Do you believe there are 'four corners' to the earth [Revelation 7:1], that God physically has eyes that move around the earth [Proverbs 8:17; Zechariah 4:10], or that someday a dragon will be prowling around with us [Revelation 12:3]?"

The best communication here seems to be to answer a question with a question. "Tell me," I often ask, "have you ever seen a beautiful sunset?"

"Of course," is the usual answer.

But then I must insist, "No, you haven't: you may have seen the effect of the sun disappearing over the edge of the earth as it rotated away from the sun. But you have never seen the sun set. What's the matter? Don't you believe that the earth rotates and that the sun only *appears* to 'rise' and 'set'?"

"Well, of course, that's what I mean," they answer.

"Then why didn't you say what you meant?" I persist.

"I did," they insist. "I was just using a common figure of speech."

By this time in our conversation the point I am making is clear. The use of figurative language in any type of literature does not mean that there are errors in it. Figures of speech do not constitute errors; they may in fact be the most accurate way to communicate truth. Saying the eyes of God move all over the earth is simply a good way of figuratively picturing the fact that God is everywhere and knows everything. It probably communicates better than a theologian's saying that the immanent and transcendent God is omnipresent and omniscient!

The book of Revelation is not saying that a dragon will walk the earth. Revelation is a vision of symbols that represent what will really happen. Sometimes those symbols are interpreted for us and sometimes they are not, but in either case they must be taken the way the author used them. In this case, the dragon is identified as "the serpent of old who is called the devil and Satan" (Revelation 12:9).

Figures of speech certainly do not constitute errors in the Bible.

What about the unbelievable stories? Some question the creation account of Adam and Eve, the episode of Jonah and the great fish, the crossing of the Red Sea on dry land, the raising of Lazarus from the dead, Christ's walking on the water, and so on. But those are questions of faith, not accuracy. They are not inconsistencies or errors. The historical literal reality of the Old Testament accounts of Adam and Eve as well as that of Jonah are confirmed by Jesus Christ as historical fact (Matthew 12:40; 19:4). If we choose not to believe the Bible or Christ's statements about it, that's one thing, but our not believing the Bible certainly does not make it inaccurate.

What about the Bible's violation of its own morals? Someone will say: "How can we believe that the Bible has no errors in it, when in one place God says, 'Thou shalt not kill,' and in another place God tells Joshua to kill whole populations of Canaanites?" Or, "How can the Bible say adultery is physical when Christ says it is mental?" or, "How can the Bible be without errors when it says adulteresses are to be stoned, yet Christ let the woman caught in adultery go free?"

There is no moral hopscotch in the Bible. From Genesis to Revelation the Bible reveals the completely consistent values of one and the same God. All apparent inconsistencies reflect our own lack of understanding. Almost all of us have been accused of inconsistencies by people who don't take the time to understand us. Generally, a little beyond-the-surface investigation will clear up those false notions.

In the first case mentioned here, the answer is that the command of Exodus 20:13 is "you shall not murder." It specifically uses the Hebrew word for "murder," rather than the more general word for "kill."[3]

As to the second question, adultery is physical. Christ never

---

3. Francis Brown, S. R. Driver, C. A. Briggs, *Hebrew and English Lexicon of the Old Testament* (London: Clarendon, 1968) pp. 953-54.

said it wasn't; He said only that it is also mental. And contrary to what the legalistic Pharisees were saying, the mental lusting was also sinful. There is no contradiction here but rather a clarification and application.

As for adultery's requiring the death penalty—it did. Christ never contradicted that or any other part of the law (Matthew 5:17). But He also claimed to be God (John 10:10; 14:9; 17:5). As God, He had the power to forgive. Being forgiven of a sin does not mean the thing committed was not a sin. Christ never said that the woman did not really sin or that she was not guilty enough to be stoned to death. His point was that He, being God, could forgive her. In a similar way we might forgive our children for disobeying, even though we have not changed our view of their action as being wrong.

What about contradictory statements in the Bible? The accusation that the Bible contains contradictory statements generally deals with statistics. For example, in Genesis 15:13 God predicts that the Israelites "will be enslaved and oppressed *four hundred years*," yet Exodus 12:41 reads, "And it came about at the end of *four hundred and thirty years* to the very day, that all the hosts of the LORD went out from the land of Egypt." Also, Mark 5 and Luke 8 describe one Gerasene demoniac who confronted Jesus, whereas Matthew 8 says there were two. Matthew 28:2 mentions only one angel at Christ's tomb, and John 20:12 says there were two. Mark 6:8 speaks of the disciples taking staffs along on their journey, but Matthew 10:9-10 seems to speak against it. Also, Luke's genealogy of Christ differs from Matthew's. The accusation is that the Bible must have errors in it because certain statistics are different.

Again, a closer examination reveals that these statistics are not contradictions at all. Sometimes number discrepancies, like the years of the Egyptian bondage, result from an author's speaking of a general rounded-off figure in one place but an exact one, "to the very day" (Exodus 12:41), in another. In other cases one author begins his counting from a different point in time from that of another.

In the case of two demoniacs versus one, and two angels at the tomb or one, that is certainly no contradiction. If there were two, there certainly was one. There were, no doubt, many angels, and a hillside full of demoniacs (since that is where their society forced them all to live). One author simply mentions two, whereas the other zeros in on one. The Bible never says there was *only* one demoniac or *only* one angel.

Concerning taking a staff (Mark 6:8) versus not having one (Matthew 10:9-10), a closer reading will solve the supposed problem. In Mark 6 Christ instructs them to only take along "a mere staff," whereas in Matthew 10 He tells them not to "acquire" an additional one. In Mark the instruction is on what to *take along*, but in Matthew the instruction is concerning what they were not to *acquire* after they got going.

The difference between the genealogy of Jesus presented in Matthew and Luke is solved by a similar closer look at the text. Matthew describes Joseph's heritage; Luke describes Mary's. Obviously, then, they differ after their common ancestor King David.

Any book as large and complex as the Bible, which deals with as many crucial intellectual, spiritual, and moral issues as it does is going to make statements that will not be obviously understood with a surface reading. Many apparent problems appear as we study its text. This is true any time we study anything beyond what we already understand. But a lack of understanding is certainly not a contradiction or an error in the text.

WHY DO I HAVE TO DECIDE?

Mr. Briggs wanted to know why the every-word-accuracy of the Bible was a subject he needed to make a decision about. This is probably the most important decision a Christian can make, after he has decided to receive Jesus Christ as his personal God and Savior. Logically, it is not even possible to decide to make Jesus Christ the Lord of our lives until we have decided that the record of His commandments is word-for-word accurate. He said, "If you love Me, you will keep My commandments" (John 14:15). But how can we do that if we have not decided that the written record we have of those commandments is without error? If there are any mistakes at all, then we are left to ourselves to decide which parts are right and which are not—in which case *we*, not Christ, are the masters of our lives.

But this decision is not restricted just to the gospel accounts of Christ. It is a "first of all" decision we must make about the whole Bible. The apostle Peter wrote that we must decide to "know this *first of all*, that no prophecy of Scripture is a matter of one's own interpretation, for no prophecy was ever made by an act of human will, but men moved by the Holy Spirit spoke from God" (2 Peter 1:20-21).

In the previous context Peter talks about how he and the other apostles were "eyewitnesses" of the Lord (v. 16). He confirms that they personally heard words from God the Father confirming Christ's glory (vv. 17-18). But notice something interesting from the context. Peter's defense of his message is not all this personal revelation, or the fact that it works, or even Peter's own experience, but rather that his message is true to Scripture—the accurate, completely error-free, written Word of God. Therefore Peter calls his readers to believe him.

Since the Bible is the very breath of God, as Paul told Timothy in 2 Timothy 3:16 (the Greek word for "inspired" means "God-breathed"), we have a sure and certain word from the Almighty Creator of the universe by which we can confidently live.

5

How Do I Know Whose Interpretation Is Right?

It was a rainy night. But that didn't seem to keep them away. Doctors, factory workers, college students, lawyers—it seemed everybody but Indian chiefs began driving up. They huddled under umbrellas and slushed their way through the dark into a large Memphis home. Most of them had never been there before, but they were about to experience a most unusual party.

Once inside, the door was closed on the dreary night, and the atmosphere was warm with Southern hospitality. The hum of voices and the smell of hot coffee drifted from the dining room where a table was heaped with every kind of hors d'oeuvre and dessert imaginable. For example, if you like dip, there were green dip, yellow dip, brown dip, hot dip, mild dip, and baskets full of things to dip with. There were punch, coffee, cake, pies, cookies, and lots of friendly people of various ages eager for conversation.

More significant than the difference in the ages and occupations of all those guests were the differences in their beliefs. There were Jews, Hindus, Buddhists, reincarnationists, various breeds of liberal and conservative Christians, and one fellow who was into astrotravel (floating in and out of his body). If you were to go around the house meeting people, you would find that the only thing they all had in common was that they all seemed to have absolutely nothing in common.

About 8:00 the host asked everyone to come into one room and said he'd like to have a fifty-nine minute and fifty second discussion about religion—"Life and God" he called it. Well, you

63

might expect them all to leave at that point, but believe it or not, that's why they came.

A man named Ben led the discussion. He had barely finished reading a quote about the Bible when a lady in a yellow dress said, "The Bible according to whom?"

Squinting to read the lady's name tag, Ben asked, "What do you mean, ah—is it Gloria?"

Gloria smiled, nodded approval at the recognition of her name, then answered, "I mean, everybody interprets the Bible differently. My husband is Jewish; I grew up in a Protestant Christian church; and my children are Unitarians. If you quote something from the Bible around my house, you've really got a discussion on your hands. Everybody thinks it means something different. How do you know who's right?"

"Well, first of all, I'd just take it at face value," Ben answered. "What's the biblical statement in question most apt to mean, taken in its most normal sense? I call that taking it *literally*. Second, I'd check the context around it to see what it's talking about."

"True," Gloria broke in, "that helps sometimes. But other times that just isn't enough."

"I know what you mean," Ben agreed. "We all understand things from different mind-sets. We come to the Bible or any other piece of literature with a whole background of thoughts and feelings, and we tend to get the meaning we bring to it rather than the one intended."

"So how can you ever know what it really means?" asked a college girl perched on a stool in the doorway.

"I think the key is to try to learn the thoughts and feelings of the author who wrote it," Ben suggested.

"You mean God?" interjected an older man, thoughtfully stroking his chin.

"Yes," Ben continued, "but also the human author God used to write it."

"Now you take my son, for instance," Gloria broke in. "He

thinks 'Thou shalt not kill' means it's OK for him to refuse to go to war. My husband disagrees, and I really don't know."

"Well, after all, killing is a big part of war," observed a young man, fidgeting with a little marble horse he had picked up from the coffee table.

"I don't think the Bible means to say that we should not go to war," suggested a rather proper-looking middle-aged lady.

"Well, Gloria," Ben broke in, "how could we use what I suggested earlier to solve this one?"

"Let's see—" Gloria paused thoughtfully "—we should take it at face value, check the context, and try to figure out what the author had in mind when he wrote it."

"Excellent!" Ben answered enthusiastically. He looked around the room as he continued. "Each of us has different beliefs, thoughts, and feelings. But when we bring those to a particular passage of any literature, we don't stand much chance of understanding it." Then he looked at Gloria and said, "The question of understanding the Bible is not 'What do you believe from your Protestant Christian background?' nor is the question 'What does your husband believe from his Jewish background?' nor your children with their Unitarian background. The question is, What did the author of the Bible mean? What did he believe about what he said, considering his background?"

"That sure is a different way to look at it," Gloria admitted.

"When you've done those three things," Ben continued, "consider a fourth. Plug the passage into the bigger context of the whole Bible. Ask yourself, 'When does it occur, and what was God saying at that particular time?'"

UNDERSTANDING THE BIBLE

Let's slip out the back door of the discussion party for now.

Ben gave Gloria four specific answers to her question. Here's a closer look at those answers.

INTERPRET THE BIBLE LITERALLY

The first thing to keep in mind when studying the Bible is that it is not less than normal literature. It is, of course, more than normal—in that it comes from God—but it is not less than normal. Therefore, it is to be understood, first of all, literally. It's not necessary to approach the Bible with some unique mystical idea. We need only to accept it at face value—in its common, ordinary, regular sense. That's what I mean when I say it must be interpreted literally.

Literally means normally.

When you find figures of speech, take them as figures of speech, because that's normal. If we are reading a poetry book like Psalms or Proverbs, then we must read it as poetry. If we are reading some book of the Bible that is telling us about history (like Genesis or Acts), then we must understand it as history. If we are reading a parable, then we must take it at face value as a parable.

If after reading a portion of the Bible we simply ask ourselves, "What is the most normal way to understand this?" we will be well on our way to arriving at its intended meaning.

INTERPRET THE BIBLE "IN CONTEXT"

The next key to an accurate understanding is to plug a passage into its context. Here is a handy rule of thumb: *The smaller the context considered, the greater the possibility of a mistake;* conversely, *the larger the context considered, the less the possibility of a mistake.* The reason, of course, is that when only a small piece of the text is used, the possibility of meanings is great, whereas when a large portion is studied, only a few possibilities could meet the conditions of the larger discussion.

One word could mean many different things. The question that must ultimately be answered is not, What does a particular word mean in different contexts? but, Which of those meanings is being used in this particular context?

As an example, what do you think I mean when I use the word

"hose"? You might think of any number of things. What if I add a second word and say "water hose"? Now you know I do not mean ladies' stockings, but there are still many possibilities of meaning. If I add a third word and say "fireman's water hose," you not only know I was not referring to ladies' stockings, but that I was also not referring to the water hose in my garden. The more of my words you consider, the fewer options there are for what I mean, and the smaller the chance that you will make a mistake in understanding me.

The same is true with a statement in the Bible. Every word is in a phrase, which is in a sentence, which is in a paragraph, which is in a chapter, which is in a book, which is in either the Old or New Testament, which is in the Bible.

As we study a particular passage, we must force ourselves to withhold judgment on what it means until we have read what precedes it and what follows it.

Many of those involved in the cults have confused people about the meaning of a particular passage of Scripture by violating the principle of context. First they attempt to set our minds to thinking according to the doctrine of their particular cult. Then they show us a verse in the Bible that sounds like it says what they have tried to program us to believe. So the context they want us to plug the verse into is the one they have built in their conversations with us, not the one offered by the Bible. That technique seems quite convincing, and the cults have used it to lead many astray.

Before deciding what a particular verse means, check *its own* context. What is the meaning of the paragraph in which it is located? What is the point of the chapter and the book itself?

INTERPRET THE BIBLE ACCORDING TO WHAT THE AUTHOR HAD IN MIND

Besides approaching the Scripture in a normal, literal manner and considering the context of each passage, a third question is crucial to interpretation: What did the author mean to say?

Here, for the first time in our discussion of interpretation, we run into a situation that is unique to the Bible.

Every book of the Bible has two authors—God, and the human being He inspired to write it. God's personality and purpose can be seen throughout the Bible, providing a unity of message from Genesis to Revelation. But His personality and purpose is recorded without error by a human author, whose personality and purpose can also be seen in the books he has written. To understand the Bible we must understand God. But to understand any particular book in the Bible, we must understand the human author God used to write it. Since God did not keep the personality of the human author out of what he wrote, we can assume that God wants us to understand the point the way the human author understood it.

That does not mean that the human author was always right about everything he ever thought or said. But it does mean that he was right about his understanding of what he wrote in the Bible. It may be, for instance, that the apostle Paul thought that Jesus Christ was coming back during his own lifetime. If he did,

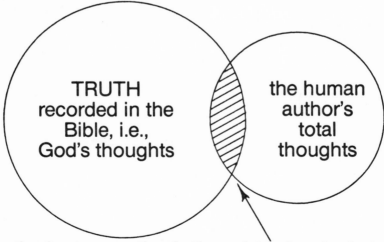

TRUTH recorded in the Bible, i.e., God's thoughts

the human author's total thoughts

the human author's thoughts about what he wrote in the Bible

he was wrong. But if he did, he never said that in the Bible. So Paul may have been wrong about some of the things he thought, but his thoughts were not wrong about what he wrote down in the Bible.

So a major factor in understanding anything written in the Bible is an understanding of the mind-set of the human author of a particular passage as it is derived from that passage.

Much of the time the author of the book is known because his name is given either in that book or somewhere else in the Bible. But even when we do not know for sure who the author is (as in 1 and 2 Kings and Hebrews), the principle still applies. We need not know who the author is—only what his mind-set was about what he has written down. And we can determine that from what he wrote, even if we do not know his name.

The author's mind-set or thoughts in a given passage can be determined by considering three things:

1. The author himself—when we know who he is
2. The author's audience
3. The author's situation

A good summary of that information is readily available in a good study Bible, like *The Ryrie Study Bible*,[1] or a good one-volume commentary, like *The Wycliffe Bible Commentary*.[2]

The author himself. Each human author of the Bible had a unique personality, and God used that in communicating what He wanted us to know. For example, the gospel of Matthew comes into focus when we get to know Matthew. Matthew was the Jewish tax collector Levi. As such, he was undoubtedly a keeper of detailed records. Since tax collectors were known for being crooked, he also was likely known as a sinner. The Pharisees, the conservative religious leaders in Matthew's time, held them-

1. Charles Caldwell Ryrie, *The Ryrie Study Bible* (Chicago: Moody, 1978).
2. Charles F. Pfeiffer and Everett F. Harrison, eds., *The Wycliffe Bible Commentary* (Chicago: Moody, 1962).

selves up as examples of righteousness. They also held that tax collectors, like Levi, were examples of unrighteousness.

When Levi (whose name was changed to Matthew) became a believer in Jesus Christ, several things probably stood out in his mind:

1. Since he was a Jew with a Jewish heritage, he would be likely to notice Christ's development of the Jewish laws and prophecies.
2. Since he was a tax collector, he would be conscientious about keeping and presenting detailed records of Jesus Christ's genealogy, sermons, and teachings.
3. Since *Matthew* was called unrighteous by the Pharisees, and Jesus called *the Pharisees* unrighteous, we should expect Matthew to emphasize true righteousness—which I believe is the subject of his gospel.

So Matthew's *thoughts* are an important preface to his gospel.

The author's audience. When we write a letter, the person to whom we write it has a lot to do with what we mean by the particular words we use. If I say, "We'll have lots of fun," in a letter to my mother, I mean something entirely different than if I use those same words in a letter to my nine-year-old daughter.

The same principle is true for the authors of the books of the Bible. James wrote his letter in the late A.D. forties to a practically all-Jewish church, which at that time probably never seriously considered the probability of any significant number of Gentiles becoming Christians. Paul wrote in the A.D. fifties and sixties, especially in Galatians and Romans, to an audience trapped in the heat of the Jew-Gentile struggle of the early church. John wrote his epistles in the A.D. mid-nineties to a church that had long since settled the Jew-Gentile issue but was then being plagued by the gnostic cult (which said Jesus was less than God and that it did not matter how one lived, just so he had the right philosophies). A feel for those audiences paves the way to an understanding of how God used those authors.

The author's situation. Psalm 51 is a beautiful piece of Hebrew poetry. But if you read it without knowing the author's situation, you will miss much of what he is saying.

May I ask you to do something? Stop reading this chapter, dog-ear the page of the book, and read Psalm 51 before you continue. Don't read on until you have read that psalm.

Have you read it?

If you have, now read and consider carefully the superscription to the psalm: "For the choir director. A Psalm of David, when Nathan the prophet came to him, after he had gone in to Bathsheba." (By the way, this is not just an editor's comment but is part of the original Hebrew text David recorded.)

Remember the situation? It is recorded in 2 Samuel 12. David committed adultery with Bathsheba, made her pregnant, and then murdered her husband by having him sent to the front lines of battle. Then Nathan, God's prophet, came to David and told him (by using an illustration) how displeased God was with his actions. David then realized his sin; heavy-hearted with guilt, he prayed Psalm 51.

Now read the Psalm again.

What a difference it makes: Our understanding of David's words improves considerably when we know something about the situation he was writing from.

So a picture of what was going on in the author's head is crucial to understanding the meaning of what he wrote.

INTERPRET THE BIBLE ACCORDING TO PROGRESSIVE REVELATION

There is another key for unlocking the meaning of a passage. The question is, Where does it occur in the Bible? God did not tell us everything He wanted us to know all at once. He revealed it slowly over more than fifteen hundred years. So where each book fits into that progress of revelation is crucial in understanding and applying it.

When God has revealed crucial doctrinal issues like salvation, spirituality, maturity, and things about Himself (e.g., His love and sovereignty), there is, of course, no change from one age to the next. There may be less revealed or only certain aspects revealed in the earlier books, but there are no changes. All the facts fit together to form the perfect whole.

But when it comes to how God wants people to manage themselves, the commands differ from one age to the next. Not that God is different, but the amount of His revelation available to man is different. Some specific commands will remain the same. But some change.

Consider, for example, Leviticus 19. In verse 18 God tells the Israelites, "You shall love your neighbor as yourself." Is that a command for us today? Of course it is! Christ repeated it for us to follow in Matthew 22:39, as did the apostle Paul in Galatians 5:14. We can conclude, then, that this is valid for all ages, because everything we know about God demands it. From the relatively small amount the Israelites knew to the tremendous amount we can know, the requirement to love our neighbors as ourselves is clear.

But not every command stayed the same. Let's go back to Leviticus 19. The next verse reads, "You shall not breed together two kinds of your cattle; you shall not sow your field with two kinds of seed, nor wear a garment upon you of two kinds of material mixed together" (v. 19). Is it wrong today to mix cattle, grain, or cloth? Are Herefords, Holsteins, Angus, and other beef cattle sinful? Is it sinful to sow wheat and another grain together, or to wear clothing made of cotton and polyester? Of course not! Why not? Because God did not give us those commands for today. They were part of the Mosaic law, which was discarded as an administrative structure when Christ died on the cross (Romans 10:4; Galatians 3:23-25).

So why did God tell them to do those things? Remember,

the only written revelation they had was Genesis and Exodus. When everyone rejected God at the time of Noah and again at the Tower of Babel, God said the world could best learn about Him by what He did for Israel. That included the Israelites' being obviously different from those around them. Apparently mixing cattle, grain, and cloth were things practiced by the nations that followed pagan gods, and the God of Israel wanted His people to be obviously different. Different revelation required a different set of administrative practices. Some of that "different set" is the same as today, and some of it isn't.

But then, changing rules is not so unusual, is it? When we raise our children we do not require the same things of our three-year-olds that we require of our thirteen-year-olds. Nor do we give the same instructions to our thirteen-year-olds as we give our eighteen-year-olds. Why? Because we have changed? No! It's because *they* have changed—because of the amount of knowledge they have acquired. God has done the same with us.

There are several places in the Bible where God gives a new set of administrative practices, accompanying new revelation. It might be helpful in your study of the Scriptures to know where some of those administrative divisions are. Here are a few general ones:

- Genesis 1-3—Adam before the Fall
- Genesis 4-8—From Adam until the Flood and Noah
- Genesis 9-11—From Noah until the confusion of languages at Babel
- Genesis 12-Exodus 19—From Abraham to the Egyptian bondage and Moses
- Exodus 20-Acts 1—From the law of Moses to the death and resurrection of Christ
- The gospels and Acts-Revelation 19—The church, the Body of Christ today

- Revelation 20—The future one-thousand-year reign of Christ on earth
- Revelation 21-22—The eternal state

Remember! This is *not* to say that only Acts through Revelation 19 and the gospels are for us today. *All* the Bible is for us today.

God has revealed Himself as much, if not more, in the Old Testament as in the New. To neglect the Old Testament would be to neglect part of God's essential message, which He has commanded us to know and use (2 Timothy 3:16). The point that is being made here is that those *administrative* laws that were given for specific periods in the progress of revelation should be understood in the larger context in which they were given and not pulled out of that context.

An accurate understanding of the Bible is not difficult. But it does take some effort. Be careful not to take on a mind-set of some group or some point you want to prove before you go to the Bible. Keep trying to ask, "What is the author of the text trying to say? What is the passage he wrote talking about?" not, "What do I want it to be talking about?" Then apply those four ideas, and you will be well on your way to an accurate understanding of the Bible.

6
Does God Do Miracles Today?

"Yoo-hoo! Anybody home?"

"Come on in, Betty. I'm in the kitchen," Sue called out with a scratchy, half-awake voice.

"Am I too early?" Betty asked.

"Not at all," Sue assured her. "I sure do appreciate your willingness to help clean up. How about a cup of coffee?"

"Sounds great."

"What do you take in it?"

"Black is fine."

"Good. I don't think I could find the cream and sugar in this mess, anyway." Sue shoved various dishes aside to find a place to put Betty's coffee cup on the counter.

"Well," Betty sighed, watching Sue cross-piling dirty dishes. "That was a terrific party last night. You and Frank went to a lot of trouble and expense to get all the neighborhood together. The least I can do is help you clean up."

The women moved to the dining room table to wake up with their coffee before getting started.

"Is everybody gone already?" Betty asked. "It's only eight thirty."

"Frank is still asleep," Sue answered. "He usually doesn't go to the store until ten thirty or so, because he gets home so late. But the kids have all gone to school."

"Don't you have a son in a Bible college?" Betty asked.

"Uh-huh. Johnnie just started this year."

"Well, maybe you can answer a question I've been wondering

about." Betty's voice took on a more serious tone. "My Robert is in his senior year of high school. Last week he came home and announced that he wanted to go to Bible college. Well, that sounded fine, but he doesn't know which one he wants to go to. He's got information from several different ones. And, boy, they sure are different!"

"How do you mean?"

"Well—" Betty paused cautiously before she answered "—it's the stuff about visions and faith healings. You know—miracles. Some places say they aren't for today, and some make them sound like the definition of Christianity. What do *you* think?"

"Oh, I think it makes sense to believe that God can do miracles all right," Sue began. "I mean, after all, if God is a supernatural being, then He sure can do supernatural things. On the other hand, we don't have to assume that God does not do natural things. Sometimes I get the feeling that lots of Christians don't believe God does anything naturally. After all, if He created nature, why not expect Him to work within the natural systems He set up?"

"Hm." Betty drummed thoughtfully on her coffee cup. "Then why do you think God did the miracles recorded in the Bible? I mean, some of those sure go against the natural laws He set up. Like, why did He walk on water and raise people from the dead?"

"It seems to me those things were done to show that some particular message or messenger was from God," Sue answered.

"You mean God had Jesus do miracles to show that He was His Son?" Betty asked.

"Yes, I think so," Sue called from the kitchen where she had gone to get the coffeepot. "What I mean is, that's what I think the Bible teaches," she continued, as she carried the coffeepot back to the dining room.

"Well, let me ask you this," Betty began. "Whoa! That's plenty, thanks," she interrupted herself as Sue refilled her cup. "Do you think God is doing those supernatural kinds of miracles today?"

"The last chapter of the Bible says that nobody is supposed to add to the Bible until Jesus comes back," Sue answered. "If there isn't going to be any more Bible revealed, then there is no reason to expect any more miracles, either—that is, until Jesus comes back."

"Yeah. But couldn't God do some miracles of that beyond-nature sort today if He wanted to?"

"Oh, sure," Sue acknowledged. "And He certainly doesn't need to check with me before He does it! But on the other hand, for me to say that some vision or healing or something done today is of God would be another story. I'd be saying God is doing something different from what He did in the Bible because the visions and healings God did in the Bible accompanied His revelation. In other words, I would be going beyond the Bible. I don't want to ad lib when it comes to what God is saying and doing."

MIRACLES TODAY

Let's add some details to the six issues Sue and Betty considered.

ARE MIRACLES REASONABLE?

Of first importance to our understanding of the question of miracles is that they are reasonable, not just mystical. If there is a God as described in the Bible, then what would appear as supernatural to us may be natural to a superior being.

Let me fantasize a little bit to illustrate.

Once upon a time a flower and a dog were sitting out in the hot sun.

"Sure is hot out here!" exclaimed the flower.

"Sure is," the dog agreed, "but that's no problem. I'll just go sit under the shade of that tree over there."

"You can't do that!" said the flower.

"Sure I can!" argued the dog. And he got up and moved over under the shade to prove it.

"That's a miracle!" the flower concluded.

Now let me break away from my story for a minute and ask,

Was that a miracle? Well, it would be if the flower did it, but not when the dog did it. Why not? Because the dog is a different kind of being than the flower.

Back to the story.

The dog got bored under the tree, so he went into the house and asked his master if they could go hunting tomorrow. "First I'll check the weather report," the man said as he sat down and studied the weather page of the newspaper. "Yep. It's going to be good hunting weather tomorrow," he said. The dog then looked at the newspaper. He sniffed it. He chewed on it a bit. But he learned nothing about the weather from it.

"That's a miracle!" the dog concluded.

Was it a miracle to get the weather report from the newspaper? It would be if the dog did it, but not when the man did it. Why? Because the man is a different kind of being than the dog.

So they went hunting and shot a duck, but it fell down into the water. "Oh, rats!" the man exclaimed. "Now we'll have to get wet in order to get our duck."

But God came along and said, "No. I'll just walk out on the water and get it for you."

"That's a miracle!" the man exclaimed.

Now I ask you, Was that a miracle? Well, it would be if the man did it, but not if God did it—if indeed He is a different kind of being from man.

The moral? Miracles are reasonable actions of a superior being.

ARE THERE DIFFERENT KINDS OF MIRACLES?

There are two situations to which we often attach the same word—miracle. But the events are actually significantly different. One is the type of event that is contrary to the laws of nature as we observe them in our three-dimensional world. Those we will call *supernatural*. The others are events that are contrary to the laws of probability but are not contrary to the laws of nature. We shall call these events *superprobable*.

Supernatural events are not just wonders of nature that could be ultimately explained by further scientific research. They are things that simply could not happen naturally. These supernatural events include things like walking on water and raising people from the dead. I do not mean using some trick or invention that could cause us to walk on water. I mean walking on it with our bare feet or with sandals, as Jesus and Peter did. I do not mean resuscitation of people declared clinically dead by medical definition. I mean raising someone who is dead and rotting in the grave so that his body is stinking like Lazarus's was (John 11:39). Those events are clearly supernatural. And the Bible clearly states that God gave power to perform those events during the time the Bible was being written.

Superprobable events include things like accurately predicting seven years of plenty and seven years of famine, or being released from prison by an earthquake. These are also events accomplished by God. They are clearly contrary to any laws of statistical probability, but are not violations of any observable laws of nature.

It must be emphasized that superprobable events are no less significant nor any less of God than the supernatural ones. I am reminded of the old story of the farmer who fell off a haystack in his barn. As he plunged toward the floor, he prayed, "Lord, save me!" As he fell, his suspenders caught on a nail and stopped his fall, saving his life.

"Never mind, God," he then prayed. "My suspenders saved me."

Answered prayers do not cease to be important when carried out superprobably instead of supernaturally. Why should we insist on God's going beyond the natural laws He set up in the first place?

WHAT IS THE PURPOSE OF SUPERNATURAL EVENTS?

Observations from Scripture lead to the conclusion that supernatural events accompany new revelation. The purpose of these events seems to be to verify revelation as indeed being from God and not just from men. Supernatural events are most prominent during three historical periods:

1. Moses
2. The Old Testament prophets
3. Christ and the apostles.

But those periods were also the times of the greatest revelation. Moses wrote the first five books of the Bible; the prophets wrote the last seventeen books of the Old Testament; and the apostles (or those they sanctioned) wrote the New Testament.

The Lord Jesus Christ was the greatest agent of supernatural events. Nearly every time He healed someone, for example, the healing was contrary to nature. But Jesus was also the greatest agent of revelation. The supernatural events were a testimony that He was indeed the Messiah.

When John the Baptist was put in prison, he apparently began to wonder whether Jesus was really the Messiah or not. So he sent some of his disciples to ask Him about it. Jesus responded by pointing to His supernatural activity as proof of who He was. He told John's disciples,

> Go and report to John what you have seen and heard: the BLIND RECEIVE SIGHT, the lame walk, the lepers are cleansed, and the deaf hear, the dead are raised up, the POOR HAVE THE GOSPEL PREACHED TO THEM. [Luke 7:22]

The supernatural events were to be an authentication to John that Jesus was indeed the Messiah (see also John 20:30-31). The purpose of Christ's supernatural work was not to create faith in people but to provide evidence that He was revealing truth from God.

God did not give us the whole Bible at once. He did it over a period of many years. As He revealed something, He often accompanied that revelation with supernatural works. He did not always use supernatural events to verify revelation, but every time He did use such events, it was in one way or another to authenticate some revelation.

This purpose is also given in Hebrews 2. After warning us to not "... neglect so great a salvation," the author goes on to say, "After it was at the first spoken through the Lord, it was *confirmed* to us by those who heard, God also *bearing witness* with them, both by *signs* and *wonders* and by *various miracles* and by gifts of the Holy Spirit according to His own will" (Hebrews 2:3-4, italics added). Again we see that the supernatural works had the purpose of *confirming* revelation from God.

DO SUPERNATURAL EVENTS CONTINUE TODAY?

Since supernatural events seem only to be used in the Bible to verify revelation from God, we must first answer the question, Does revelation continue today? When the Old Testament ended, it looked forward to new prophecy (i.e., revelation) from God. Because the New Testament is completely in harmony with the morals and doctrines of the Old Testament (and neither are paralleled in any other writing), it is safe to conclude that the New Testament is indeed that additional prophetic revelation. But when the New Testament ended, God emphatically declared there would be absolutely no additional revelation given until Jesus Christ comes back again. Revelation 22:18 reads, "I testify to everyone who hears the words of the prophecy of this book: if anyone adds to them, God shall add to him the plagues which are written in this book." When God finished revealing the last book of the Bible, He had said all He was going to say and all we need to know until our Lord returns.

Therefore, since God is not giving additional revelation today, we cannot remain consistent with the Bible and say God is performing supernatural events today. It would be consistent with the Bible to say God *could* do supernatural things today, but not that He *is* doing them.

As we see the time of God's revelation drawing to a close in the

New Testament, we see a gradual decreasing of supernatural events. Christ's ministry was filled with the supernatural. So was the ministry of the apostles at first. In the gospels and the early chapters of Acts we can find a supernatural event on nearly every page.

By the time we get to the middle of Acts, however, we may have to turn several pages in our Bibles before we come across anything supernatural. By the time we get to the end of Acts, there are very few of those events. While reading the epistles written toward the end of that first century, we are hard pressed to find anything we have here described as supernatural. God's supernatural activity seems to be centered on His revelation of Himself to the apostles and the others who wrote the New Testament.

One of the surest signs a religious activity is *not* of God is that it claims to have new revelation. One characteristic of nearly every cult is that it claims to have received a modern word from God. Such groups are generally begun by a cult leader who supposedly received a new supernatural message. Interestingly enough, he or she often claims to do miracles of the supernatural type.

The apostle Paul tells us that these extrabiblical religions are from Satan (1 Corinthians 10:20) and that they will increase as we approach the "later times" (1 Timothy 4:1). Satan also has the power to work supernatural events (Exodus 7:8-15). Satan, of course, would love to deceive people into worshiping him while they think they are worshiping God (Isaiah 14:12-14). He would certainly glory in deceiving people by giving their cult leader some "new message" plus the accompanying supernatural abilities.

I want to make *clear*, however, that I am *not* saying every group that believes God is doing the supernatural or giving new revelatory visions today is of Satan. Many godly, born-again Christians also believe this. I understand their position, acknowledge their experience, and recognize them as brothers and sisters in Christ. I must simply say that I find no parallel for their experience in the Bible.

The only way we can be *sure* any idea is from God is if it is consistent with the Bible. The idea of new revelation added to the Bible is clearly inconsistent with God's revealed Scripture.

COULD GOD DO SUPERNATURAL MIRACLES TODAY?

If we ask, "Is God *able* to do supernatural events today?" the answer is, "Of course He is." God is able to do anything that does not violate His own character. The more relevant question is not Could He? but, Is He?

If our commitment is to know about God only what the Bible knows, then we could not say for sure whether any supernatural event performed today is of God.

My personal decision is to know nothing more about God and His work than the Bible knows. If someone tells me that he saw a vision or performed a supernatural work, I can acknowledge his statement as something I know *about*. But if he asks me if I think his vision or supernatural miracle is from God, I do not have the freedom biblically to say that it is or that it is not. If God wants to do something supernatural today, that is clearly up to Him. But for us to comment on such activity as being God's is to go beyond the authority God has given us—the Bible.

WHAT ABOUT SUPERNATURAL HEALING?

An intriguing example of someone who has researched supernatural healing is William A. Nolen, M.D., who did a survey of the "healing" ministry of Kathryn Kuhlman. He writes,

> In talking to these people, I tried to be as honest, understanding, and objective as possible, but I couldn't dispense with my medical knowledge and my common sense. I listened carefully to everything they told me and followed up every lead that might have led to a confirmation of a miracle. I was led to an inescapable conclusion: Of the patients who had returned to Minneapolis to reaffirm the cures

claimed at the miracle service, not one had, in fact, been miraculously cured of anything.[1]

I, too, am prepared to state categorically that I have never, ever seen any healing that was contrary to nature.

I have pursued this subject with doctors and theologians and have never found anyone who could show me a supernatural event of any kind. I have, of course, heard a multitude of stories and read many books and articles that claim supernatural miracles. But none of those authors or conversationalists were ever able to show me one.

I am sure that many of my Christian friends consider me to be extremely limited and unfortunate. I would simply say that I have heard these stories for years, and I have not heard a new type of story in a long time. I have investigated every type of story and have yet to find anything appearing to be supernaturally of God.

As an example, all types of cancer have been known to be healed by themselves. It is very unusual, but it happens, and it happens with unbelievers as well as believers. Someone who prays to be healed of cancer and gets well is, no doubt, healed by God. But that is not supernatural; it is superprobable. God regularly uses natural means to heal people—beating all the statistics of probability.

On the other hand, I have heard about people preaching the gospel in a real existing language that they did not know and someone in the audience understanding it in that language. If that is true, is it of God? It may well be! As I said, God is able to do that if He chooses to. (Although I have never seen any such experience verified.) Therefore, if someone is asking *me* if that event is of God, I do not have the freedom to say that it is, because it goes beyond my biblical authority.

If we hear about an event that is clearly supernatural, unable

1. William A. Nolen, "In Search of a Miracle," *McCalls* (September 1974), p. 106.

to be called superprobable, and not clearly satanic, then all we have biblical authority to say as Christians is, "I don't know what its source is." God certainly does not need our permission or endorsement for what He does.

On the other hand, He *has* given us the things He wants us to give direction on. (If a man wants to know if his affair with another man's wife is of God, I can give him a clear word from the Scriptures on that—Exodus 20:14; Matthew 5:27-28; Luke 16:18; Romans 13:13). But spiritual preoccupation with things He has not commanded us to be involved with is clearly not biblical.

7

Can We Lose Our Salvation?

"Kathy, it's time to get ready for bed."

"Oh, Mom. Can't I just watch the rest of this program?"

"Kathy, that's on for another hour."

"No, it isn't."

"Yes, it is, Kathy."

"Mommmmmmm!"

"KATHY: Get your teeth brushed and your jammies on—*NOW*."

"Every time I want to do something, I have to go to bed. I never get to do anything," Kathy's voice trailed off as she disappeared into the bathroom and slammed the door.

It may not actually have been harder to get Kathy into bed when her father was out-of-town, but it sure seemed like it to her mother. With both mother and daughter tired from battle fatigue, the mission was eventually accomplished. Kathy was finally in bed, teeth brushed, pajamas on, and ready to pray with her mother.

"Dear God, please be with Daddy on his trip and Lisa spending the night at Linda's house. I'm sorry I talked back to Mom and kicked Billy in the stomach today. And Jesus, please come into my heart and save me again. Amen."

Then her mother prayed. She almost did not say what she was thinking. But then, just before hug and kiss time, she said, "Kathy, I'm real glad you told God that you were sorry, and the most important thing you can do is ask Jesus to come into your heart, but Jesus doesn't leave you when you are bad."

"He doesn't?" Kathy seemed surprised.

"No, honey," her mother continued. "When Jesus comes into your heart, He never leaves you."

"But what if I am real bad?" Kathy wanted to know.

"Well, then Jesus feels *real* hurt that you would disobey Him. But He doesn't leave you. The Bible says you are born again when you trust Christ. You can never be unborn, can you?"

"I guess not," Kathy admitted.

"You and Lisa were born into our family. If you disobey Daddy or me, we feel bad, but you will always be our daughters. It's the same when you are born into God's family by trusting Christ."

"Then what should I do if I am ever bad again?" Kathy asked.

"Tell Jesus you are sorry, and thank Him for forgiving you and paying for that sin on the cross," her mother answered.

"OK," Kathy answered, as she threw her arm around her mother's neck for a hug.

Actually, Kathy's mother was thinking about a little longer discussion, but the six-year-old's mind had taken all the theology it was going to for one night. However, let's think a little more about the question raised by Kathy's prayer. Here are five aspects of that question she will confront as she gets older.

The Security of Salvation

HOW ETERNAL IS SALVATION?

The most obvious fact about our salvation as dealt with in the Bible is that it is not usually referred to as "salvation," or even being "born again." It is most frequently referred to as "eternal life." The Greek word for "eternal" (*aionios*) means forever— something without beginning, something without end, or something everlasting. This word is used to define salvation at least fifty-two times in the New Testament. Thirty-seven of those times it is translated "eternal," and fifteen times it is translated "everlasting" (according to the King James Version). Here is a list of those verses for your future study.[1]

- Matthew 19:16, 29; 25:46
- Mark 3:29; 10:17, 30
- Luke 10:25; 18:18, 30
- John 3:15-16, 36; 4:14, 36; 5:24, 39; 6:27, 40, 47, 54, 68; 10:28; 12:25, 50; 17:2-3
- Acts 13:46, 48
- Romans 2:7; 5:21; 6:22-23
- Galatians 6:8
- 1 Timothy 1:16; 6:12, 19
- Titus 1:2; 3:7
- Hebrews 5:9; 6:2; 9:12, 14-15
- 1 Peter 5:10
- 1 John 1:2; 2:25; 3:15; 5:11, 13, 20
- Jude 21

God describes the position we have in Him, through receiving the Lord Jesus Christ as our personal God and Savior, as *eternal* life. If God saw our salvation position as something we could lose, He surely chose an unlikely word to describe it. And He used it fifty-two times.

HOW MUCH DOES THE BIBLE SAY ABOUT THE ETERNAL NATURE OF OUR SALVATION?

The eternal nature of our salvation is no minor subject in the Bible.

Jesus said, "And I give eternal life to them, and they shall *never* perish; and *no one* shall snatch them out of My hand. My Father, who has given them to Me, is greater than all; and no one is able to snatch them out of the Father's hand" (John 10:28-29, italics added).

---

1. *The Englishman's Greek Concordance of the New Testament* (Grand Rapids: Zondervan, 1970), p. 20.

He also said, "All that the Father gives Me shall come to Me, and the one who comes to Me I will *certainly not* cast out" (John 6:37, italics added).

He told Nicodemus that he had to be born spiritually. One certain thing about anyone born to us is that he is always our child. He may be good or bad, love us or hate us, stay with us or leave, but he is forever our child.

The apostle Peter said that we are born again "to obtain an inheritance which is imperishable and undefiled and will not fade away, reserved in heaven for you" (1 Peter 1:4).

Paul reminds us, "There is therefore now no condemnation for those who are in Christ Jesus" (Romans 8:1). Then he goes on to say, "For I am convinced that neither death, nor life, nor angels, nor principalities, nor things present, nor things to come, nor powers, nor height, nor depth, nor any other created thing, shall be able to separate us from the love of God, which is in Christ Jesus our Lord" (Romans 8:38-39).

Here is a more complete list of references for your future study:

- Numbers 22:12; 23:19
- 1 Samuel 28:19
- Psalm 23
- Malachi 3:16
- John 1:12; 3:3; 4:13-14; 5:24; 6:37; 8:28; 10:28-29; 14:16; 15:3; 17:2, 11-15
- Romans 3:28; 4:4-6, 16; 5:1-2, 7-9, 20; 6:4-6; 8:1, 11, 35-39; 16:25
- 1 Corinthians 1:2; 3:15; 6:19; 12:13; 15:49
- Galatians 3:29
- Colossians 2:10; 3:3
- Ephesians 1:13; 2:8-9; 4:30
- Philippians 1:6
- 1 Thessalonians 5:23-24
- 2 Timothy 1:9, 12; 2:14
- Titus 3:5

- Hebrews 10:14; 13:5
- 1 Peter 1:3-5; 3:18
- 1 John 2:1; 5:13
- Jude 24

IF SALVATION IS A GIFT, CAN I GIVE IT BACK? WHAT IF I STOP BELIEVING?

Some gifts can be given back, and some cannot. If I give my daughter a new bicycle and she abuses it, I could take it back. But that is not true of all gifts. It depends on the nature of the gift.

Suppose I give her a polio vaccination. That is a gift she cannot give back. If after I give her the medication she refuses to believe in polio vaccinations and even denies that she ever got one, is she still vaccinated against polio? Of course she is! Why? Because the nature of the gift will not allow it to be given back or destroyed—even if she stops believing in it. The references listed above tell us that salvation is just such a gift. It depends not on us but on God. It is a gift that God calls "eternal."

The Bible nowhere tells us that we are to keep ourselves saved. It is, of course, very important to understand that a holy life is a constant struggle. Our sin hurts God tremendously (Ephesians 4:30) and causes us great grief in this life and a loss of rewards in heaven (1 Corinthians 9:18, 27). But our salvation position before God is something eternal, accomplished by God at the moment we trust the Lord Jesus Christ for forgiveness of our sins. Paul says we are to "work *out* [our] salvation with fear and trembling" (Philippians 2:12). But we are *not* told to work *toward* it or work *to keep* it.

Of all the major world religions, biblical Christianity is the only one that teaches that we cannot lose our salvation. It seems natural for man to feel that he needs to maintain his position before God, because all other religions see salvation as a work of man. Obviously, if man must be or do something to get right with

God, then he would stop being right with God when he stopped being or doing those things.

For example, many believe that we would not lose our salvation for doing something "a little sinful" (i.e., lusting, gossiping, or coveting), but we would if we stopped believing or joined a satanic cult. (By the way, I want to make clear that many of the people who believe that are truly born-again Christians and sincerely living a godly life. I simply wish to point out that they are in error about this point—not that they are "bad guys.") What these folks are actually saying—although they may not wish to admit it—is that we stay saved and get into heaven if our sin levels do not rise above a certain point. To them, lusting, gossiping, and coveting are, then, sort of ultimately acceptable sins, whereas disbelieving and satanism are not. But such a situation would mean that God is less than perfect, since in the final analysis He would be allowing certain sins.

The Bible teaches that no sin is acceptable. Sins aren't just forgiven; they are paid for. People may be forgiven of their sins, but sin itself must be paid for. Either we accept the payment Jesus Christ made on the cross, or we will have to make the payment ourselves (Matthew 8:12; Revelation 20:11-15). If God just forgave sin by overlooking it, then Christ would not have had to die. But He did. And when He did, He paid for all the sins of all time. We could not possibly commit a sin He has not already paid for, and if we have received Him (John 1:12), then all our future as well as past sins have already been wiped off our record (Isaiah 1:18).

Salvation is *not* an effort on the part of the believer to not sin. Salvation is a cleansing of all sins of all time totally accomplished by Christ on the cross (2 Corinthians 5:19-21) and applied to the believer at the time he or she receives Christ.

Can a Christian stop believing? Of course he can! But he cannot stop being saved. Why? Because that sin like all sin is already paid for and removed from him. Of course, it is very likely that when a person has stopped "believing," it is because he or she never trusted Christ in the first place. Anyone in a state of disbelief should never assume he is saved because of some previous experience. The only point made here is that *if* he really was saved (and only God would know that), then he is always saved. Again let me emphasize, we should never assume a person is saved because of some previous religious or emotional experience.

The point is, the believer still has a sin nature which is capable of all the same sins it was capable of before he was saved. Of course, God will discipline a Christian (Hebrews 12:5-11), and the indwelling Spirit will convict him (John 16:8), and that normally means less sin over a period of time. But it is possible for a Christian to commit any sin that a non-Christian can commit (Romans 7:14-25; 1 John 1:8-10). The difference is that the payment for those sins has already been made and applied to the Christian.

WHAT ABOUT THE UNPARDONABLE SIN?

The expression "the unpardonable sin" is in one sense like the expressions "Cleanliness is next to godliness" and "God helps those who help themselves." The one thing all such expressions have in common is that not one of them is in the Bible. However, many sermons have been preached, questions asked, and booklets written on the question of the "unpardonable sin."

The Bible mentions a sin committed by the Pharisees that Jesus called "blasphemy against the Spirit," adding that, for whoever did what they did, "it shall not be forgiven him, either in this age or in the age to come" (Matthew 12:31-32; Mark 3:28-30; Luke 12:10).

A couple of observations are significant to understanding the "blasphemy against the Spirit" as seen in Matthew 12. For one thing, the "blasphemy against the Spirit" is nowhere repeated in the Bible. The apostles never warned anybody about it, nor suggested it as something that could be done. They were very specific in their warnings and exhortations to the early church, careful not to overlook anything that the Body of Christ was to be or not be. But they never warned anybody against an unpardonable "blasphemy against the Spirit."

A second observation to consider here is that there are two different kinds of events described in the Bible. There are the ones that might be repeated anytime (like someone praying) and the ones that will probably never be repeated (like the Israelites crossing the Red Sea on dry land).

Some sins are unique to a certain time. For example, after Joshua captured Jericho, the Israelites were told not to take anything out of the city (Joshua 6:17). Is it always sinful for a conquering army to take things out of the city they have conquered? No, but it was sinful with that city at that particular time. The consequence was also unique. Anyone taking anything from Jericho was to be "burned with fire" (Joshua 7:15), along with his whole family. Does that mean everyone who steals should be burned up, and his family as well? No, because that was a sin that could only be committed at a particular time in history.

The sin of Matthew 12 appears to be just such a sin.

The issue in this passage is, Who is Jesus? Is He the Messiah (John 8:24), or a blasphemer (Mark 2:7)? To blaspheme the Spirit was actually to see Jesus in a human body doing miracles by the power of the Holy Spirit and to reject that as evidence that He was the Messiah, the God of Israel (John 8:24). This sin was committable while Jesus was physically on earth doing those things. After that, the conditions for this particular unpardonable "blasphemy against the Spirit" were (and are) not present.

Therefore, it could not be committed today.

WHAT ABOUT THOSE PASSAGES IN THE BIBLE THAT SEEM TO SAY WE CAN LOSE OUR SALVATION?

Suppose a friend says to you, "I think a person could lose his salvation if he's bad enough. What do you think?" Then you answer, "Well, I'm really not sure. Do you know any verses that would support that?" And he says, "Yes, I do." Then he turns to one in the Bible.

Now let me ask you a question. "What subject are you thinking about as you look at the verse with your friend?" Well, generally, you are thinking about salvation and, specifically, whether or not you can lose it. The passage may not be discussing salvation at all. But if you take the verse your friend pointed out and plug it into the subject on your mind (in this case, salvation), you may not get the meaning intended by the Bible.

In order to understand what the Bible means, we must see its words in the context of the author's mental image, not ours.

If a passage of Scripture is to teach us something about whether or not we can lose our salvation, it must of course be in a context that is talking about salvation. So here is an important question. What things would we expect to find in the context, if it dealt with salvation? One thing would be the blood of Christ—His death on the cross as a substitute for our sins. Another would be our receiving that payment through faith so that we might stand before Him blameless. But we can be sure if there is no mention of these things in the passage, it is not dealing with salvation—let alone how to lose it.

The problem with lack of security is one of misunderstanding God's purpose for writing the Bible. God did not write the Bible just to get people saved. Our salvation is only a necessary means to an end. The real end, or purpose, for which God wrote the Bible was to reveal Himself to us so that we might be godly, or righteous. His desire is for man to stop sinning and practice holiness (Matthew 5:48; Ephesians 2:10; 1 Peter 1:16). God talks about more in the Bible than salvation. He also tells us *why* He saved us. Obviously, if we bring a mental context of salvation to every passage we read, we are going to misunderstand many of them.

In Appendix 1 of this book I have included a brief discussion of ten passages commonly used to say we can lose our salvation, as well as an explanation of that passage taken in its context.

The eternality of our salvation is no picky minor point to be left to the theologians. It is a basic, biblically crucial issue that will affect our thinking as well as little Kathy's. It will not only affect our thinking about our salvation, but it will penetrate our understanding of much of the rest of God's Word as well.

8

Is Everything Predetermined, or Do We Have Free Will?

"To the left, more to the left!"

"Aren't we gonna hit that rock?"

"No. We'll miss the rock, but we need to get far enough to the left to hit the center of the trough."

The two canoers listened for a few seconds, as the threatening roar of the falls ahead of them increased. Jake's thoughts rushed back to the warning given them by the outfitters.

"Stay in the center and paddle hard," the instructor had said. "This is the most dangerous falls on the river right now, so hit it straight. If you roll over, hang on to your canoe. If you lose the canoe, take a deep breath, because you'll go under—life jackets and all. Twenty-five seconds later you'll pop up. Take another deep breath. Don't fight it, because she'll suck you back down for another thirty-five seconds, then spit you out downstream. We've timed it, and it does the same thing every time."

Jake's thoughts were interrupted by Pat's voice. "We're drifting to the right again," he yelled from the front end of the canoe.

"We're awful close," Jake answered, "and the rapids are really picking up. Do you think we should chance moving over this close?"

"I think we'd better," Pat returned.

Neither of them were what you would call expert canoers, but they were experienced enough to know it was a dangerous move, especially with the Guadalupe River as high as it was—higher than they had ever seen it. As a matter of fact, their group could only find one outfitter willing to rent canoes to them today.

"OK. Straighten it out. *Straighten it out!*" Pat screamed.

Too late. The rapids grabbed the canoe and rolled it like a log. Jake saw Pat fly out the right side, and the next thing he knew he was underwater, being rolled and turned by the boiling current. It seemed like more than the twenty-five seconds the outfitter had said, but sure enough, up he came. He could see the back end of the canoe in front of him, just beyond his reach. He took a deep breath, and back down he went for what seemed like an eternity. Just about the time he thought his lungs would burst, he came up in the rapids, about fifty yards downstream from the falls.

That night there was lots of conversation around the campfire. Everybody sounded very brave—now that it was over and they had all survived the experience. But Pat's comment was probably the most intriguing of all.

Remembering the Bible study Jake had led the night before on God's sovereignty, Pat said, "Say, Jake. I wonder if that decision we made to move to the left of the falls was God's predetermined plan or our choice."

"I'd say it was both," Jake offered.

"Both! That's dumb," Pat complained. "If God has everything planned out, then we didn't really make a mistake, because we didn't actually decide anything. On the other hand, if *we* decided to turn left, then *we* are responsible for turning over."

"I know," Jake answered. "But the Bible says both are true. It tells us God controls everything—so there are no accidents. But it also tells us we have a real responsibility for our choices. From God's point of view, there are no accidents, yet *we* make mistakes."

"How can that be?" Pat wanted to know.

"Well, if God is really infinite, eternal, and all that, then maybe it's just beyond our understanding," Jake answered.

"Are you saying God's not reasonable?" Pat asked.

"He's not *less* than reasonable," Jake answered. "But He is *more* than reasonable—to our knowledge, anyway."

"Yeah, but," Pat insisted, "if everything is predetermined,

then it's already settled who's going to be in heaven and who isn't. How can *that* be fair?"

"We have to remember," Jake began, "that God has done what He has because it's best *overall*. The plan that built the road through those trees over there wasn't the best plan for the trees that had to be cut down, but it was done because it seemed to be the best plan overall. Since God always sees the best ultimate good, His plan is best overall."

"So you think little things like the way we steer the canoe are in God's plan?" Pat wanted to know.

"Sure," Jake admitted. "If something is not in God's plan, then He is not a completely sovereign God. Besides, how do we know a little thing might not cause some bigger thing? If we hadn't rolled over just the way we did, maybe we'd have gotten hurt real bad."

"Then how can you say we are responsible?" Pat wanted to know.

"The same way I know we are in God's plan," Jake answered. "The Bible says so. We have real responsibility, and we are held accountable to God for what we do."

"How about prayer?" Pat asked. "Why should we pray, when God's going to do whatever He's planned to do, anyway?"

"For the same reason," Jake answered. "We also have an ability to choose. The Bible doesn't describe us as just a bunch of puppets, chanting out the lines written for us by a God holding all the strings. We are also personal beings making individual requests of a concerned Creator."

PREDESTINATION AND FREE WILL

Let's break away from the canoe trip. Pat asked some challenging questions. They fit into three broad categories:

1. Can both predestination and a real choice be possible?
2. Did God preplan everything?
3. Do we have an unhindered ability to choose?

Here are other facts to consider in answering those questions.

CAN BOTH PREDESTINATION AND A REAL CHOICE BE POSSIBLE?

Let me expand an illustration I used in my book *Answering the Tough Ones*.[1]

As I sit here writing, my paper is lying on the top of a flat desk. The surface of the desk has no depth to it at all. Now suppose this flat plane on my desk top were extended all over the room and it was inhabited by flat, two-dimensional people. Let's say they are as intelligent as people anywhere but they are flatlanders living in this two-dimensional land.

Suppose I write a note to the flatlanders and tell them that I, a three-dimensional person, exist and that, while sitting at my desk, I am both above flatland and below it at the same time. I am also in it as my body penetrates through it. They would no doubt say, "Huh?"

Next, suppose I attempted to explain that I am five feet nine inches tall and weigh one hundred sixty-three pounds and that they could see me by looking at me sitting at the desk. They may look and see the rather silly shaped oval that my body makes as it penetrates flatland, scratch their heads and ask, "What's a 'tall'? For that matter, what's a 'pound,' and why do you have a hundred and sixty-three of them?"

Is God understandable? The more we would talk, the more the flatlanders would be confused with apparent contradictions. We would talk about different things that are reasonable in themselves, but they would never add up together in the minds of the flatlanders. Ultimately, they could only make sense of it all by believing I existed, since they could only know the parts about me that I could reveal to their understanding. They would have to conclude that the apparent contradictions of reason would

1. David A. DeWitt, *Answering the Tough Ones* (Chicago: Moody, 1980), p. 30.

somehow be reasonable only if they could see things in the unknown third dimension of which I spoke.

God is a being far greater than we are. He commands as many dimensions as He wishes, and the difference between Him and me is far greater than that between the flatlanders and me. In the Bible, God tells us many things about Himself that are beyond our understanding. He tells us that He is three and yet one, and that He became man in Jesus of Nazareth in such a way that Jesus was 100 percent perfect man and 100 percent God at the same time (without, of course, being 200 percent). He also tells us that He has completely planned everything that will happen, yet we have an unhindered ability to choose.

Is God reasonable? "But," we insist, "that's logically impossible — it's not reasonable!" Well, of course, if God is a beyond-three-dimensional, infinite, eternal being, then what He says would indeed be reasonable, if we could see it from His perspective.

The evidence for the fact that these things are indeed from God is that they are not unreasonable but superreasonable. They are not less than reasonable, but they are more than reasonable.

The difference between a contradiction and an apparent contradiction is that the contradiction violates logical thinking, whereas the apparent contradiction does not. Instead it goes beyond logical thinking. Nothing God tells us is illogical, and it is right to approach the Bible reasonably and logically. Everything God tells us about His sovereign plan is reasonable. Everything He tells us about our ability to choose is reasonable, too. But when we attempt to put the two together, it goes beyond our understanding. So although God's Word is more than reasonable, it is not less than reasonable.

Doesn't this illustration I heard explain it? Be careful with illustrations that try to tie together God's sovereignty and man's free will. There is a tendency to use illustrations that diminish one side or the other. For example, a pilot told me recently that he "understood this predestination/free will thing." He explained that as he flew at several thousand feet he could see roads, cars going down those roads, and the things they would come across as they went. He was able to determine their future, in a sense, because he had a different vantage point to look from. At the same time, the people in the cars had the ability to do whatever they chose to do.

But his illustration is a poor one. It illustrates God's prior knowledge all right, but not His plan. It would only illustrate God's sovereign plan if my pilot friend had built the road, then built the cars and the people in them. He must also have preplanned for those cars and those people to be going down that road at that particular moment, coming across the things they came across exactly as it happened. He would also have had to design to the last detail every thought and action of everyone in every car, including every decision each driver made. On the other hand, this would illustrate man's free will only if the people in the cars were completely free of any design by anyone and could choose whatever they wished.

The important thing to remember is to keep from watering down one truth for the sake of the other.

DID GOD PREPLAN EVERYTHING?

Now let's consider separately God's preplanning and man's free will choice. First, God's plan.

Are there any accidents? Everything that takes place is in God's plan, and everything in God's plan takes place—exactly as He planned it. The Bible records Job's saying to God, "I know that Thou canst do all things, and that no purpose of Thine can be thwarted" (Job 42:2).

In 2 Kings 19:25 God says, "Have you not heard? Long ago I did it; from ancient times I planned it. Now I have brought it to pass."

Isaiah 14:24 reads, "The LORD of hosts has sworn saying, 'Surely, just as I have intended so it has happened, and just as I have planned so it will stand.'"

Revelation 17:17 explains the action of the godless forces preceding Christ's second coming by saying, "For God has put it in their hearts to execute His purpose . . . until the words of God should be fulfilled."

There is no such thing as an accident. Everything is part of God's purpose, and all His purposes are carried out.

God's all-encompassing plan includes our salvation. Ephesians 1:4 states, "He chose us in Him before the foundation of the world." The next verse says, "He predestined us to adoption as sons." The conclusion of the passage is, "In Him also we have obtained an inheritance, having been predestined according to His purpose who works all things after the counsel of His will" (Ephesians 1:10-11). In Acts 13:48, Luke records, "As many as had been appointed to eternal life believed."

Our very decision to receive Christ is the result of a time of God's calling us through various events in our lives. As Romans 8:30 says, "Whom He predestined, these He also *called*" (italics added).

If we neglect the concept of God's complete sovereign plan we must cross lots of verses out of our Bibles. Here is a list of a few of these. I include it here just to show the magnitude of this concept in the Bible.

- Genesis 18:25
- Exodus 14:17
- Numbers 23:19
- Deuteronomy 29:4; 32:39
- Judges 9:23
- 1 Samuel 2:25; 16:14
- 2 Samuel 12:11
- 1 Kings 22:23
- 1 Chronicles 10:14
- Job 12:15; 14:5; 42:2
- Psalm 33:10; 47:7; 69:6; 75:6; 104:14, 28; 135:6; 145:17
- Proverbs 16:4
- Isaiah 4:35; 10:5-23; 14:24; 40:12; 44:18; 46:9-10; 53; 55:11

- Jeremiah 15:2
- Daniel 2:21; 4:17
- Amos 9:7
- Nahum 1:3
- Habakkuk 1:6
- Matthew 10:29
- Luke 12:7; 22:22
- John 6:44; 12:40
- Acts 2:23; 4:27-28; 12:23; 13:48; 15:18; 16:14
- Romans 8:29; 9:20-21
- 1 Corinthians 1:26-31
- Ephesians 1:4; 3:11
- Philippians 2:13
- 2 Thessalonians 2:13
- 2 Timothy 1:9
- 1 Peter 2:8
- Revelation 15:8; 17:17

Is it fair for some people not to be in God's plan to be saved? In Romans 8 and 9 Paul develops the idea of our position before God as believers in Christ. He says we can be secure in our salvation because God chose us and predestined us to be saved. Then he anticipates our question of how fair that is to those not chosen. He says, "You will say to me then, 'Why does He still find fault? For who resists His will?'" (Romans 9:19). Paul goes on to answer that question by giving an illustration in which God is like a potter making pottery and people are the various different vessels being made by God. He writes,

> On the contrary, who are you, O man, who answers back to God? The thing molded will not say to the molder, "Why did you make me like this," will it? Or does not the potter have a right over the clay, to make from the same lump one vessel for honorable use, and another for common use? [Romans 9:20-21]

But we do not like that answer. Our generation is taught that we are the highest creatures in the universe and humanity is all-important. The Bible agrees that we are important, but not just in and of ourselves. We are important because we are important to God.

Sometimes I raise a little garden of mostly tomato plants. I water and care for the garden, but I also hoe out the weeds that grow in it. Often when people come to visit, I show them my garden. I have never had anyone tell me that it was unfair of me to hoe out those weeds and leave the tomatoes. Why not? Well, because the garden was made in the first place for the benefit of me—not the weeds or the tomatoes. Those tomatoes are valuable, not because they are valuable in and of themselves, but because they are valuable to me.

I realize that the situation we are discussing is far more complex than the tomatoes and weeds in my garden. But then it is also true that the greatness of God compared to me is far more than the greatness of me compared to my tomatoes. We are indeed His creation in His garden, made for the purpose of His honor and glory—not ours! We are valuable not in and of ourselves, as modern humanistic thinking would have us believe, but because we are valuable to God. Whatever brings about His glory is the highest good.

Did God plan for me to stub my toe? The Lord Jesus Christ said,

> Are not two sparrows sold for a cent? And yet not one of them will fall to the ground apart from your Father. But the very hairs of your head are all numbered. Therefore do not fear; you are of more value than many sparrows. [Matthew 10:29-31]

In the same way that God is sovereign over sparrows and the hairs of your head, He is sovereign over everything.

Suppose a housewife on the way out the door to get groceries stubs her toe while getting her children ready. She sits down for a few seconds to rub it a bit until at least some of the pain goes away.

Insignificant? Perhaps. But perhaps not.

What if that few seconds' hesitation causes her to be just enough behind her original schedule so that a moving van going down the street will have passed, which otherwise would have hit her broadside, seriously injuring one of her children? To say God controls moving vans and the well-being or injury of children but not the stubbing of toes may be inconsistent.

The Bible does not teach fatalism—whatever is going to happen is going to happen by any means—but the controlling hand of a personal infinite God. So all the "little" *means* are as much a part of the plan as the "big" *ends*. A God who is not sovereign over all is not really sovereign at all.

Ephesians 1:11 tells us that God "works *all things* after the counsel of His will" (italics added).

Why did God include bad things in His plan? Ultimately, we can not know why God does everything He does. As a matter of fact, He scolded Job fiercely for trying to figure it all out (Job 38-39). Moses wrote, "The secret things belong to the LORD our God, but the things revealed belong to us and to our sons forever, that we may observe all the words of this law" (Deuteronomy 29:29). So we must concentrate on what God *has* revealed, not what He has *not* revealed.

God has told us, however, that not all of His wishes are included in His plan. He does not want us to disobey, yet our disobedience is a fact of His plan. God is "not wishing for any to perish but for all to come to repentance" (2 Peter 3:9; see also 1 Timothy 2:3-4), yet His plan includes many who will indeed perish (Revelation 20:11-15).

In a much simpler way, we can see that in our own lives. We wish we could do things today that we do not plan to do. Also each day we plan to do things that we would really rather not do.

Why do we plan to do those things? Because we believe that to be the best possible plan for the day. Consequently all *our* desires are not in *our* plans, either.

DO WE HAVE AN UNHINDERED ABILITY TO CHOOSE?

Now let's look at the other side of the coin—our ability to choose. As much as we find God's sovereign hand working on every page of the Bible, we also find man's ability and responsibility to choose.

Are we responsible for our actions? If there is anything clear from the pages of Scripture it is that man is responsible. Adam and Eve were cast out of the Garden of Eden because they were held responsible for their sinful choice. The old prophet Samuel told the disobedient King Saul, "The LORD would have established your kingdom over Israel forever," but he also told him that God was not going to do that, because "you [Saul] have not kept what the LORD commanded you" (1 Samuel 13:13-14).

"Choose life," God told Israel, "in order that you may live" (Deuteronomy 30:19). Their life depended on their choice.

Faith in Christ is also seen as a matter that involves choice. "EVERYONE WHO CALLS ON THE NAME OF THE LORD SHALL BE SAVED," Peter told the crowd in Jerusalem (Acts 2:21). Jesus said that "whosoever" believed in Him would have everlasting life (John 3:16). The offer of salvation to *"whosoever"* would choose to receive it is repeated throughout the Bible (see Acts 10:43; Romans 10:13; Revelation 22:17).

After concentrating on God's sovereignty in Romans 8 and 9, Paul turns to an emphasis on man's choice in Romans 10. He says, "If *you* confess with *your* mouth Jesus as Lord, and believe in *your* heart that God raised Him from the dead, you shall be saved" (Romans 10:9, italics added). In the next verse he says that "righteousness" comes about when *"man* believes." He goes on, then, to reason, "And how shall they preach unless they are sent? Just as it is written, 'HOW BEAUTIFUL ARE THE FEET OF

THOSE WHO BRING GLAD TIDINGS OF GOOD THINGS!'" (Romans 10:15). The implied answer, of course, is that people will come to faith in Christ only if other people make a willful decision to go and tell them about Christ.

Do we choose to love? One of the key concepts of the Bible is that of love. We are commanded to love one another (John 13:35), to love God, and to love our neighbors (Matthew 22:37-39). But love is impossible if we do not have a real ability to choose *not* to love. We cannot choose to love our husbands, wives, children, parents, friends, or anyone unless we have a real ability to choose not to love them. If God's control were such that it limited man's ability to choose, then we could never really say, "I love you"—not even to God. If we got to heaven without making a real independent choice, we could never love God, but only see ourselves as controlled computers in God's machine. Our ability to make choices is essential for nearly every command in the Bible.

Can we pray for changes? Prayer is another area where our ability to choose is crucial. God did not tell us that our prayers were just insignificant chants programmed into us by a controlling God who had the results all worked out anyway. Instead He commands us to "pray without ceasing" (1 Thessalonians 5:17). He says, "The effective prayer of a righteous man can accomplish much" (James 5:16). But He also tells us to pray persistently (Luke 11:1, 5-10), thankfully (Colossians 4:2-4), and many other ways which require responsible choices (see John 15:7; 16:23-24; 1 Peter 3:7, 12; and 1 John 5:14). After Moses prayed, in Exodus 32, we read, "*So the* LORD changed His mind about the harm which He said He would do to His people" (v. 14, italics added). A choice is essential for carrying out God's instructions on prayer.

Can we believe in both predestination and an ability to choose? Not only does God tell us that He is in complete sovereign control over everything at the same time that we can make real choices, but He also mentions both concepts together in His Word.

Speaking of His betrayal by Judas, Christ said, "For indeed, the Son of Man is going as it has been *determined;* but woe to that *man by whom* He is betrayed" (Luke 22:22, italics added; see also Jeremiah 18:1-2; John 6:37, 44, 65, cf. vv. 29, 35, 40, 47; Romans 1 and 10; cf. Romans 8-9).

God has told us all that we need to know to live the life He wants us to live to glorify Him. He has not told us everything there is to know about those topics or even everything we would like to know. When a cook bakes a cake, she puts in just the right amount of sugar and flour. If the cake is a good one, it will not contain all the sugar or flour available to the cook. It will have just the exact amount needed for that particular cake. So, into His recipe for the abundant life He has designed for us, God has put just the amount of knowledge we need, concerning both His sovereign control and our ability to choose.

Our assignment? We are to know what He has given us, deal with that information reasonably, and apply it to our lives. All the rest "belongs to the LORD our God" (Deuteronomy 29:29).

Appendix 1
Passages Used to Demonstrate Non-Security

The following is a brief discussion of ten passages commonly used to say we can lose our salvation. In the left-hand column is a passage used to prove the doctrine of non-eternal security. In the right-hand column is a brief explanation of that passage in its context.

PASSAGES USED TO SAY
SALVATION CAN BE LOST

EXPLANATION

John 15:1-6
"I am the true vine, and My Father is the vinedresser. Every branch in Me that does not bear fruit, He takes away; and every branch that bears fruit, He prunes it, that it may bear more fruit. You are already clean because of the word which I have spoken to you. Abide in Me, and I in you. As the branch cannot bear fruit of itself, unless it abides in the vine, so neither can you, unless you abide in Me. I am the vine, you are the

If we are to believe that this passage says we can lose our salvation, we must first determine that it deals with salvation—but it doesn't. Nowhere does it speak of the blood of Christ paying for our sins, our receiving Him, or any of the issues involved in salvation. The context deals with spiritual fruit, not salvation.

The passage is in the middle of the Upper Room discourse (John 14-16) Christ gave to the apostles. In the branches; he who abides in Me, and I in him, he bears much fruit; for apart from Me you can do nothing. If anyone does not abide in Me, he is thrown away as a branch, and dries up; and they gather them, and cast them into the fire, and they are burned."

previous chapter He promised them salvation. But now He is telling the same apostles that their assignment is to produce fruit. He explains that if they are not doing that, God will take away their ability to be fruitful (a condition that fits lots of Christians today). If they are fruitful, God will trim their lives in such a way that they can be even more fruitful. In verse 3, Christ says that they are "already clean"; that is, He is now not talking about salvation. Verse 6 emphasizes the point that they could become as unfruitful as a burned up branch if they did not "abide" in Christ. To read this passage as a threat by God that we could lose our salvation is to miss the whole point of it.

Galatians 5:1, 4
"It was for freedom that Christ set us free; therefore keep standing firm and do not be subject again to a yoke of slavery. . . . You have been severed from Christ, you who are seeking to be justified by law; you have fallen from grace."

Notice again that this passage contains nothing that describes salvation—no mention of the blood of Christ, His payment for our sin, or our faith to receive Him. Those who teach that salvation can be lost often use the terms "severed," "justified," and "fallen from grace" to refer to salvation. But the context says, not so: the "grace" that is being fallen from here is not salvation, but the grace of God needed for maturity. Paul was writing to the Galatians, who were being mistaught that now that they were saved they needed to keep seeking to be justified (declared right) by keeping the law of Moses. The point Paul was making was that they could not mature by continuing to live under the Mosaic law or any other law when God was dealing in grace. That life-style severed them from the abiding imput of Christ.

As Christians we must be careful not to get into the same boat as those Galatian believers. By following our own laws we sever ourselves from the imput of God's grace. This passage warns us about losing our spiritual growth, not our salvation.

Hebrews 6:4-6
"For in the case of those who have once been enlightened and have tasted of the heavenly gift and have been made partakers of the Holy Spirit, and have tasted the good word of God and the powers

These verses refer to people who are already saved, not to how those people get saved or stay saved. If the passage were talking about salvation (as people who think you can lose your salvation suppose), then it would of the age to come, and then have fallen away, it is impossible to renew them again to repentance, since they again crucify to themselves the Son of God, and put Him to open shame."

not be making the point that it is possible to be saved then lost. The point it would be making is that it is impossible to be saved—then lost—then saved again. But that's not true. The Bible clearly teaches that any living person who turns to Christ can be saved (John 3:16).

This passage, however, is not talking about getting or staying saved, as the context (5:11—6:3 and 6:7-9) clearly points out (note the words *maturity* and *things that accompany salvation*). These Jewish believers, having grown up under the Old Testament sacrificial system, thought that they had to re-sacrifice something every time they sinned. The author insists that *that* is impossible as a way of renewing one's faith after sinning. As a matter of fact, that puts Christ "to open shame," by saying that Christ's sacrifice was not good enough to cover those sins. The biblical way for a Christian to deal with sins is to *confess* them (1 John 1:9), not to offer a sacrifice for them. This passage says nothing about losing salvation. The author's point is clearly given in the first verse of this chapter when he says, "Let us press on to *maturity*" (Hebrews 6:1, italics added).

Hebrews 10:26
"For if we go on sinning willfully after receiving the knowledge of the truth, there no longer remains a sacrifice for sins."

This passage is consistent with the author's point that those who are born again in Christ are no longer part of the Jewish sacrificial system. Since Christ paid for all their sins on the cross, "there no longer remains a [temple, animal] sacrifice for sins." It is not the sacrifice of Christ, but the old sacrificial system, which "no longer remains."

Hebrews 3:14
"For we have become partakers with Christ, if we hold fast the beginning of our assurance firm until the end."

Those who deny eternal security believe this verse teaches that we will lose our salvation if we do not "hold fast" in our faith. Once again, the passage is not talking about salvation. The chapter deals with the failure of Moses and the Israelites to obey God. They did not "hold fast" and were therefore not allowed to enter the land of Canaan. If this passage taught that saved people could lose their salvation, then it would be saying that Moses lost his. But we know that's not right. Moses is mentioned in Hebrews 11 as one of God's models of faith. He also appeared with Jesus Christ on the mount of transfiguration. Moses did *not* "hold fast . . . firm until the end," yet he was certainly saved. What Moses *did* lose were some of the earthly blessings that accompany obedience. In the same way, this passage is teaching us to "hold fast." If not, we might not "become partakers" of some of the blessings Christ has for us. But saved people will not lose their salvation any more than Moses did.

Luke 14:26-27, 33-35
"If anyone comes to Me, and does not hate his own father and mother and wife and children and brothers and sisters, yes, and even his own life, he cannot be My disciple. Whoever does not carry his own cross and come after Me cannot be My disciple. . . . So, therefore, no one of you can be My disciple who does not give up all his possessions. . . . if even salt has become tasteless, with what will it be seasoned? It is useless . . . it is thrown out."

People who say that salvation can be lost claim that this passage says we can be "thrown out" of the Body of Christ. But the subject here is "discipleship," not salvation. Discipleship is the process we go through as we draw ever nearer to Christ. It may begin before we are saved (Matthew 28:19), and it continues on afterwards. Somewhere en route we trust Christ for forgiveness for all our sins, and God saves us. Jesus is here describing the ultimate goal of the process of discipleship, not the salvation decision. He says that someone who does not "calculate the cost" can lose his ability to be a disciple and become "useless" and "thrown out" as a disciple. But these verses say absolutely nothing about salvation.

Luke 8:13
"And those on the rocky soil are those who, when they hear, receive the word with joy; and these have no firm root; they believe for a while, and in time of temptation fall away."

Does this verse teach that you can lose your salvation because you can stop believing? The passage says only that you can *believe* temporarily. It does not say that you can be saved temporarily. It is a parable about the nature of faith, not about salvation. The verse is not discussing Christians or non-Christians; it is analyzing *faith*. It could be applied to non-Christians who are considering the Bible's message. They believe some of it for a while, but their worldly habits provide a great source of temptation, and they "fall away" from what little they did believe.

As mentioned previously, a believer is someone with a new nature. But we also still have our old sin natures, as long as we live in these bodies. So a believer is capable of committing the same sins as an unbeliever. If we "have no firm root" in God's Word, we may disbelieve all sorts of truth "in time of temptation." But this verse says nothing about salvation. Passages that do discuss salvation say it depends on God's promise, not on our lack of doubt.

1 Corinthians 9:27
"But I buffet my body and make it my slave, lest possibly, after I have preached to others, I myself should be disqualified."

It is often said that Paul is worried here about losing his salvation. But the context tells us that Paul is concerned about being "disqualified," not from salvation but from rewards. He says so in verses 17 and 18 of this same chapter, where he asks, "What then is my reward?" Paul consistently talks this way about rewards (see 2 Corinthians 5:10-11). He realizes that his rewards in heaven depend on his obedience here on earth. But when Paul talks about salvation he assures us he is "convinced" that nothing "shall be able to separate us from the love of God, which is in Christ Jesus our Lord" (Romans 8:38-39).

1 John 3:9
"No one who is born of God practices sin, because His seed abides in him; and he

Some people also use this verse to say we can lose our salvation. But John never suggests that our sin makes cannot sin, because he is born of God."

us unbegotten or unborn of God. He does suggest an explanation. He parallels "cannot sin" with "practice sin." To practice or do something does not mean we have arrived, but that we are working toward a certain direction. Our high school band practiced every day. Some of our band members were so bad that the only way you could tell they were band members was that they practiced music. Their membership had nothing to do with their abilities.

John says you can tell Christians because they practice righteousness (i.e., they do not practice sin). That does not mean they are good, or even better than all non-Christians. It only means that "no one born of God practices sin." We practice righteousness. We fail a lot (1 John 1:8, 10), but we continue practicing righteousness, not sin.

Romans 11:21-22
"For if God did not spare the natural branches, neither will He spare you. Behold then the kindness and severity of

Once again, this passage has nothing to do with an individual's salvation. It is a statement of the temporary nature of the church as a re-

God; to those who fell, severity, but to you, God's kindness, if you continue in His kindness; otherwise you also will be cut off."

cipient of God's blessings. Israel was grafted out as the primary object of God's blessing because of unbelief. But one day the same thing will happen to the church. Paul here warns the church that if its members become as unfaithful as the nation of Israel did, then God will graft them out just as He grafted Israel out. Fact is, that is exactly what *will* happen to the church.

Appendix 2
Fossil Evidence

1. A lower jaw and part of a skull, found near Piltdown, England, was presented by Charles Cawson in 1912. It was a fraud. The skull with teeth that had been filed down was treated with iron salts to make it look older, and the jawbone was from an ape. (Evolutionary Theory: Piltdown Man)
2. A strange-looking single tooth was found in Nebraska in 1922. Although it was used to prove evolution at the famous Scopes trial in Dayton, Tennessee, it turned out to belong to a pig. (Evolutionary Theory: Nebraska Man)
3. Along with some normal human skulls, an odd-shaped skull cap was found in Java in 1891. It was later admitted to be that of a large ape. (Evolutionary Theory: Java Man)
4. Bones that were discovered twenty-five miles from Peking in 1928 disappeared except for two teeth later ascribed to be those of a large monkey or baboon. (Evolutionary Theory: Peking Man)
5. A few odd-shaped teeth and jaw fragments were discovered in India in 1932. It has recently been reported that a baboon species in Ethiopia has the same tooth and jaw characteristics. (Evolutionary Theory: Ramapithecus)
6. An unidentifiable skull found in 1924 was later identified as being the same as the present day long-armed, short-legged, knucklewalker apes of Africa. (Evolutionary Theory: Australopithecines)
7. A supposed prehistoric skeleton discovered in the Neanderthal Valley of Germany had a brain capacity greater than the

average modern human. (Evolutionary Theory: Neanderthal Man)

8. Complete skeletons standing about six feet tall with greater brain capacity than many people today are considered to be those of prehistoric man. (Evolutionary Theory: Cro-Magnon Man)

9. Other skulls and skeletons have been identified as those of cave men, although subsequent work has shown them all to be as human as you and I. (Evolutionary Theory: Swascombe Man, Castenedolo Skull, Calaveras Skull, and Skull 1470)

The actual observations are: one pig's tooth (2, above), a few variations in ape bones (1, 3-6, above), and a few variations in human bones (7-9, above).

And that's it.

Moody Press, a ministry of the Moody Bible Institute, is designed for education, evangelization, and edification. If we may assist you in knowing more about Christ and the Christian life, please write us without obligation: Moody Press, c/o MLM, Chicago, Illinois 60610.